DAWN GROVES

MEDITATION
FOR BUSY PEOPLE

60
SECONDS
TO
SERENITY

NEW WORLD LIBRARY
Novato, California

New World Library
14 Pamaron Way, Novato, CA 94949

Cover design: Greg Wittrock
Text design & typography: TBH Typecast, Inc.

Library of Congress Cataloging-in-Publication Data

Groves, Dawn, 1955–
Meditation for busy people / by Dawn Groves.
p.   cm.
Includes bibliographical references.
ISBN 1-880032-02-3 (acid-free paper)
1. Meditation.   2. Self-actualization (Psychology)
3. Stress management I. Title.
BF637.MfG76   1992   92-12734
158' .12—dc20   CIP

First Printing, March 1993
ISBN 1-88032-02-3
Printed in Canada on acid-free paper
Distributed to the trade by Publishers Group West

20 19 18 17 16 15 14 13 12 11 10

This book is dedicated to my parents:
my mother, Eleanor,
who made me wear sweaters when she was cold,
and my father, Pappy,
who inspired me with his relentless drive to write.

Praise for *Meditation for Busy People*

"Dawn Groves takes the reader on an easy journey into the meaning, purpose, and how-to of meditation....Those who practice what she teaches will find greater harmony in life — and much more time for joyous living."
— John Randolph Price
author and chairman of The Quartus Foundation

"*Meditation for Busy People* is a brisk, business-like description of why and how someone who believes they have no time for meditation should and can begin to practice."
— *Psychic Reader*

"Both beginners and experienced meditators will enjoy this well-written and insightful book."
— *Creation Spirituality*

"Written in a pleasant conversational style, full of anecdotes and lots of good sense."
— *Small Press*

Contents

1

Getting Started

THE BENEFITS of meditation are usually cloaked in glowing abstractions such as increased balance, greater understanding, and inner peace. The purpose of this book is to turn glowing abstraction into clear, specific terminology grounded in your reality — the reality of a busy, productive, sometimes harried individual.

In these pages you'll learn the tremendous value and handy applicability of meditation. You'll find guidelines for meditative practice (known as "sitting") that take into account busy schedules, demanding lifestyles, and the need for practical applications. You'll learn a simple, powerful meditation method useful for any time frame (seconds to hours), and you'll learn how to use it under stressful circumstances. You'll also learn techniques for handling the typical, distracting problems that occur during practice time as well as how meditation affects the workplace, relationships, and leisure activities. In the back of the book you'll find two appendices. Appendix 1 contains a list of excellent reading material for further study. Appendix 2 contains a list of commonly asked questions with associated page references.

You're a busy person. You probably want to begin meditating now. This chapter provides you with all the basic information you need to get started. It briefly describes the benefits of meditation and points out unique advantages you can bring to this practice. It then covers fundamentals such as how to meditate, how much time it should take, and what kind of environment is appropriate. So, go ahead — jump in!

What's So Great About Meditation?

Meditation is probably one of the healthiest, safest, most timely, and most regenerative practices you can undertake. Far from being mysterious or abstract, meditation is directly applicable to the stresses and strains of everyday life. It is a completely nondenominational practice that has an immensely positive impact on the business of living.

It's Healthy

Meditation is very healthy for your mind and your body. Physiologically, the deep relaxation that comes with practice lowers your blood pressure, eases muscle strain, and, when combined with gentle stretching, helps release tension from your body. Psychologically, meditation teaches you tolerance and compassion, and improves your general behavior by making you keenly aware of your thoughts and feelings before you act on them. It also strengthens your concentration, enabling you to focus more clearly on any activity without excessive stress.

It's Safe

The kind of meditation in this book is completely safe. Meditation is not like being under a "spell" or even like sleeping. There's no force involved except the force of compassionate attention. There's no conjuring or invocation involved, no complicated rituals, nothing difficult. It's basically about getting to know the ins and outs of your mind. If you experience physical discomfort that disturbs you, or if you get a little light-headed, you can always open your eyes, get up, and take out the garbage. There is only one person in control of the situation and that is you. No magic here. Nothing to fear. Your safety net is the ever-present capacity to simply open your eyes.

It's Timely

In a world convulsing with general confusion and misunderstanding, the capacity to remain calm, compassionate, and insightful is urgently needed. Meditation can help you enhance these qualities through the art of nonjudgmental observation. You learn to identify destructive emotions, patterns of behavior, and reactions as they form. By identifying them, you can step aside without becoming trapped. And when you can step back from your own reaction and learn from it, you can step back from another's reaction and work around it. You then become part of the solution, not part of the problem.

It's Regenerative

With a busy lifestyle, you probably find physical and emotional exhaustion to be familiar companions. Copious responsibilities do have a way of dragging you down. Meditation teaches you how to conserve and regenerate your energy. Through the power of attention, observation, and relaxation, you can learn how to maneuver through your responsibilities with greater ease and efficiency.

The Busy Person's Advantage

You may think that your busy lifestyle is a disadvantage when it comes to starting a practice such as meditation. You may also think that meditation is only for people who live so simply that they don't have to deal with rush hour, kids, career development, health issues, and meeting the collective needs of family and friends. But guess what? You're wrong.

As a busy person, you have already developed certain qualities that will serve you well in adopting this new and beneficial practice. These qualities are curiosity, flexibility, and stamina.

1. *Curiosity*

You have a basic interest in what's going on around you. Curiosity is a way of protecting yourself against future difficulties (asking questions about the new boss, researching fuel-efficient cars, etc.). Curiosity is never idle; it encourages you to seek better ways to live and is vital to meditation. There's no room for complacency when you're beginning a new practice.

2. *Flexibility*

You can and do adapt. You may think it's impossible to change yourself or your circumstances, but that's simply not true. This world is constantly changing, and with all your responsibilities you must continually shift gears and adapt. Flexibility means that you can adjust your schedule enough to accommodate your new practice. It also means that you're likely to absorb and utilize the good habits that meditation engenders.

3. *Stamina*

You are resilient. Working a full-time job in addition to having hobbies, a social life, and maintaining significant relationships requires fortitude. It takes a lot of energy to keep on working when you feel fatigued, distracted, or frustrated. Stamina means that you won't give up easily. You'll keep practicing even through the difficult times.

In addition to having the right qualities for beginning a meditative practice, you also generate enough activity in your life to give you reason to continue meditating. The more active your life, the more opportunity you have to observe the benefits of meditation. And when you can clearly observe the rewards operating within your life circumstances, you're more likely to continue practicing and thus derive even more benefit. It just keeps getting better and better.

At this point you may want to throw your hands up in exasperation, exclaiming that your life is hectic because it can't be any other way. You have to support your family, keep up with your relationships, keep up with the house payments, and so on. If you had a choice, you'd retire and just relax. Well, that may be true, but this book isn't about wishes and what-ifs. It's about your world right now, just the way it currently is. And right now, you have everything it takes to start meditating successfully.

Why Do You Need a Method?

Whenever you learn something new, it's always best to start with a basic method, a set of steps. Following steps gives you a structure from which you can then branch out as you like. Also, if you lack experience, it's frequently easier to determine what doesn't work rather than what does. From there you can carve out your personal style, subtracting what doesn't work and adding what does.

Before learning how to meditate, understand that there are countless meditation styles. Although this book describes meditation within the structural confines of the American culture and a busy lifestyle, it doesn't mean that differing methods are better or worse. Differing methods are just different. That's all. Choice of style is extremely personal, and there are many paths up the same mountain.

In considering a meditative style, it's important not to judge one method as right and another as wrong, or to feel guilty if you find yourself attracted to a new technique. Times change. People change. Issues change. You can outgrow meditation styles like you outgrow clothes. You may meditate using one method for a year and then, finding that other styles attract you more, change to incorporate new techniques into your practice. Interestingly, just like fashion, styles of meditation will also cycle. You may decide to return to the same style you once enjoyed before, but with much greater awareness and maturity.

Keep in mind that becoming restless or bored with your meditation style might signal the need to investigate it more deeply instead of changing to something else (see Chapter 2). It's fine to experiment providing you don't use it as an excuse for not committing to a practice method.

The *Meditation for Busy People* (MBP) method described in this book is safe, portable, and economical. It can be performed while sitting, standing, or walking. And it's flexible enough to allow for variations in available time as well as for the exploration of other methods within its framework.

How to Meditate

Meditation is really an interplay of energy and attention. These dynamics are balanced using correct body posture and a meaningful mental process. As such, the aspects of posture and process are equally important.

Proper Body Posture

Before beginning your practice, you will need to learn correct body posture. Body posture is especially important because you will be spending a length of time in one physical position (unless you're walking), and if that position isn't balanced, you'll feel uncomfortable and distracted. Your body should be completely relaxed, yet awake and alert. You should also sit or walk — not lie flat. Lying down encourages a mushy mental state that slips in and out of sleep. If you experience physical limitations or back problems which make it necessary for you to lie down, try to meditate in a place that won't automatically trigger sleep. You might also try bending one or both of your arms at the elbow, reaching your hands straight up from the floor while maintaining relaxed wrists. This will exert just enough energy to keep you from snoozing. You'll know that you're falling asleep if your arms waver or drop.

The easiest, most adaptable posture is sitting with your back straight, head held high. It's helpful to stretch a little before sitting to work out tension and relax the muscles. This is particularly important before a prolonged meditation. If you're sitting in a chair, your legs should be uncrossed to avoid the potential hazard of cutting off circulation and the need to shift positions in the middle of a practice. Your arms should be uncrossed for the same reason. Some people rest their palms face up in their laps; others lightly fold them or place them flat on top of their knees. The main point is to keep your hands relaxed. If you want to sit on the floor, it's okay to cross your legs. But if you have trouble doing this, consider sitting on a thick pillow. This helps your lower back relax into a natural position and makes crossing your legs much easier. Sitting with your back flat against the wall or the side of the bed is also okay, especially if your back requires extra support.

Meditation benches provide a pleasant break

from sitting on the floor or in a chair. They're small seats that tilt slightly forward to ease back strain and allow you to fold your legs underneath them. They can be easily purchased from meditation supply catalogs (yes, mail order meditation supplies do exist), or you can make them yourself.

If you will be walking or moving in some other way, keep your neck and back relaxed but straight, and don't lock your knees. Your arms should hang loosely at your sides, and you may need to bend your neck slightly to look at the ground or your feet as you walk. It may take time to determine your best body posture. Be willing to try a few positions, and remember to be patient and kind to yourself.

The Meditation for Busy People (MBP) Method

Let's take a look at an overview of the MBP method. It's composed of three simple steps with an optional "enhancement" step:

1. *Relax*

Unwind the muscles and become physically quiet.

2. *Center*

Focus on the breathing cycle and develop the capacity to witness the mind without getting lost in it.

3. *Enhance (Optional)*

Visualize goals, focus on patience and forgiveness, or perform any other personally significant mental practice.

4. *Release*

Return to waking consciousness and reinforce the meditative experience.

Simple, but not necessarily easy.

Steps 1, 2, and 4 are intrinsic to the MBP method. Step 3 is your option to include or eliminate as time allows. It offers additional aspects such as visualizing settings and ideas, focusing on qualities like for-giveness and patience, or even comforting yourself with some form of prayer work. The meditation is effective with or without Step 3.

You can perform the MBP method while you're standing, sitting, or walking. Any form of repetitive motion that doesn't require a lot of energy or conversation can be a format under which the MBP style of meditation is possible. Each step is described below for both sitting and walking.

Step 1: Relax

The goal in relaxing is to distance yourself from your body without falling asleep. A relaxed body is unrestrained and loose. When your body is relaxed, your mind has one less distraction. Relaxing can be accomplished by directly addressing individual mus-cles, telling them to release, relax, and let go. This seems to give them permission to soften, and the body then becomes almost separate from the mind.

Relaxation procedures can be long or short, depending on how much tension you are carrying in your body and how many times you've practiced relaxing. Plan on taking a minimum of five minutes when you first start. As with most activities, the more you practice, the faster you'll see results.

If you're in a sitting position you can relax more deeply than if you're doing a walking meditation. When walking, just keep your body loose and easy. You may be carrying a lot more physical tension than is necessary to keep you upright. Releasing the extra tension won't make you fall down or cause you to trip.

Regardless of whether you are sitting or walking, the mechanics of relaxation are the same. Visualize, if you can, a wave rolling down through your body, softening and steadying each muscle as it passes on its way. If you don't think in pictures or you feel particularly distracted, try talking aloud saying things like, "My facial muscles are relaxing. My neck and shoulders are dropping. Relaxing. Releasing. Now my arms are going limp, and my hands rest easily in my lap. . . ." Continue until you've canvassed your entire body. Meditation tapes can sometimes help with this process, teaching you how to release tension and giving you self-talk to follow.

If you aren't used to relaxing in this manner, you may want to begin your practice in a sitting posture, addressing your muscles directly. Later, after you know what a deeply relaxed body feels like, you can transfer that experience to a standing or walking position. With practice, you should be able to relax your body with a quick mental sweep regardless of your body posture.

Step 2: Center

After your body is quiet and composed, begin mentally centering yourself. A centered mind is aware, alert, and focused on one thing. Centering is the core of meditation. It's the good stuff. You could stop at relaxation and still derive benefit from this process, but you'd be cheating yourself. Centering teaches you how to be compassionate with your mind and flexible with your expectations. You learn how to stick with an activity, instead of sabotaging your efforts in harsh judgment and unrealistic demands.

Centering cultivates "mindfulness," the ability to witness what is going on without getting lost in it. This is the real power of meditation — learning how to be mindful of what is actually occurring without coloring it in old memories, habits, or preconceptions. When you're mindful, decisions and responses are based on the present circumstances and not ancient history. You stop behaving like a slave to habitual reaction and unconscious, counterproductive behavior. There's room in your heart for more than automatic reaction — there's room for compassion, understanding, and new responses.

Being mindful also means you're truly present to life's experiences. You're not missing what's currently happening by wishing for yesterday or getting lost in tomorrow; your immediate experience is fully realized and understood. If the event is pleasant, like eating a fresh apple, you feel all the crisp, delicious sensations without fogging them in extraneous thought. You receive the total impact, the complete pleasure. If the event is stressful, like driving in heavy traffic, you remain sharp and alert to each change in circumstances. You're able to process information efficiently without unnecessary reaction or debilitating anxiety. You're prepared, relaxed, and not "stressed out" by the time you reach your destination.

Mindfulness increases the general pleasure of living and the efficiency of almost any action you undertake. When the mind centers, it attends to one thing, idea, or feeling — it becomes one-pointed. Every meditative practice involves some kind of mental focusing. The difference lies in the choice of focal subject. Sometimes it's a visual focus such as a candle or a cross; sometimes it's auditory such as a song or a phrase; sometimes it's physical movement such as breathing, walking, or dancing; sometimes it's the pattern of changing thoughts.

The MBP method employs the breathing cycle as a focal point for centering. Breathing is active, always changing, and ever present. No single breath is the same as the next, so there is an infinite variety of subtle sensations to observe. And the breath is convenient to use in places like an office where other focal objects may be inappropriate.

The process of centering on the breath is simple. Find a place around your nostrils or the back of your breathing passages where you can feel the rush of the breath. Feel its temperature. It comes in cool and is warm on the exhale. Feel the area of the nose where coolness and warmth change over and over again. Just be aware of it without trying to force your mind to remain tightly focused on breathing. The idea is to slide into awareness of breath. Gently. No forcing. No pushing. No anguish. Just remain present to the coming and going of breath. When the mind wanders off into distraction, simply bring it back to breathing. Return to breathing over and over. Don't get upset or angry at yourself. This isn't about force. It's about patience, tolerance, and persistence. Back to breath. Back to breath. Back to breath.

You can center on the breath whether you're sitting still or walking, but walking provides the distinctly physical sensation of taking footsteps. You may instead choose to focus on your feet. Simply walk slowly and bring your attention to the movement of each foot as it takes a step. Feel the weight shift from heel to toe as you walk. Note the movement: *bending, lifting, placing, bending, lifting, placing.* You can look down at your feet if this helps keep the focus clear. Be aware of distracting sounds or images around you, but repeatedly return your attention to the footsteps. This is a very calming practice, but it does require surroundings where you can walk with a smooth, gentle pace.

It's natural to become distracted during the centering phase of practice. Sometimes you'll catch yourself so lost in thought that it will seem like you spent all your centering time in fantasy. Just bring your attention back to breath. It is sometimes helpful to mentally say "Stop" or "Cancel" to help break the train of distraction. But don't be hard on yourself; keep returning to your focal point. Centering is a skill that develops with time.

Techniques for handling distractions are detailed in Chapter 2, "Beyond Getting Started," but briefly, you can switch from centering on the breath to observing your flow of thought. Watching the thought stream is more difficult than watching the breathing cycle. Thoughts are elusive focal points. The thought stream is a slide show of one image after another at dizzying speed. When you focus on the thought stream, you don't follow any one thought; rather, you note all the thoughts as they sail by without grabbing any picture. Imagine yourself in a movie theater noting images on the screen that are separate from you. Pretend you're watching an obscure foreign film. Just observe it without really trying to understand what it is communicating.

Going easy on yourself is very important in all centering practice because you aren't going to do this perfectly. Centering offers you the opportunity to practice a potent combination of concentration and flexibility — two keys to success in any new endeavor. Forgive your scattered attention as it displays itself, and just keep persisting. "Ooops. There I go again. Oh well, back to breath. Back to breath."

Setting a time limit on centering is somewhat arbitrary, since the whole point of this book is to introduce you to a portable practice that suits any length of time. However, when starting out in your regular set-aside time, try to spend at least five to twenty minutes on centering. You can increase the time as it feels appropriate. Meditators in retreats will sometimes spend hours in this stage.

Step 3: Enhance (Optional)

After the centering and mindfulness practice is accomplished, you can either continue into Step 4,

Release, or you can stay in a centered consciousness and play with some creative visualization practices. If you've had a rough time lately, maybe you'd prefer to work with forgiveness, loving kindness, or prayer. During Step 3 your mind is settled, your body is quiet, and you're primed for clear thinking — a good time to explore your thoughts. There are dozens of books describing different ways to investigate and expand your consciousness (just visit any New Age bookstore). The following paragraphs offer a few ideas on two powerful forms of consciousness work: creative visualization and forgiveness.

1. Creative Visualization

Many people find creative visualization to be synonymous with prayer or spiritual mind treatment. Although it can seem a little mysterious, visualization is actually a down-to-earth process with great practical application. Tennis players use visualization to practice their sport, thereby improving court performance. Speakers deliver talks in front of imaginary audiences to practice dealing with large crowds and to handle stage fright. Therapists use creative imagination to help desensitize phobic clients.

Creative visualization involves imagining certain states of consciousness, physical events, or physical conditions in your mind's eye. These events and conditions can include fulfilling goals (finishing a project successfully), experiencing desired feelings (being at ease in stressful circumstances), or enjoying uniquely meaningful settings (relaxing on a tropical island, in a forest glade, and so on). The key to effective visualization is to mentally use all the physical senses. Whatever you're visualizing, try to see, feel, taste, smell, hear, and touch it. Make it real, tangible. Feel the emotions that go with the experience such as joy, confidence, relief, peace.

Whether you are sitting or walking, the idea is to simply immerse yourself in the dream of your choice. Approaching visualization with mindfulness (from Step 2, Centering) allows your practice to become more than a delightful form of play. It frequently offers a fresh perspective, generates new insight, and clarifies issues of concern.

2. *Forgiveness*

Focusing on forgiveness is a process rich with value. In forgiveness work, you attempt to let go of anger and blame associated with yourself and others and release the heavy burden of judgment that keeps painful experiences close to you. You can then begin to experience new levels of inner peace.

Forgiving doesn't mean condoning poor behavior or compromising your values in any way. It means you acknowledge with compassion your own right or someone else's right to make mistakes — even if the mistakes are considered big ones. The fact is, you don't practice forgiveness for someone else's sake. Your hatred and blame, no matter how justified or seemingly "appropriate," doesn't hurt anybody but you. So you forgive to get on with your life and to open yourself to what the experience can teach you.

Unfortunately, motivations for unseemly behavior (yours or someone else's) can be entrenched in painful past events that you may not be consciously aware of. While therapeutically exploring the anger and guilt is useful, hating yourself or other people won't solve anything. Prolonged indulgence in hate and bitterness can't change the past; it can, however, blind you to the wisdom you might gain from the experience. Forgiveness allows for the possibility of change and makes the present less burdensome.

There are many ways to practice forgiveness. As with visualization, there are a myriad of books on the subject. Briefly, one technique is to begin by looking at pictures of compassionate beings such as Jesus, Mother Teresa, the Dalai Lama, or Gandhi. Consider their abilities to forgive and remain open to people and events in their worlds. Then bring your mind to focus on the person or action you wish to release. See yourself observing the situation as you imagine your loving role models might observe it: with empathy; with compassion for pain, insecurity, and clumsiness; with strength; with objectivity. Feel your heart open as far as it can, and then imagine the person or action floating away — released from your mind and your experience. The benefits of this technique are greater wisdom and clarity.

Focusing on forgiveness doesn't always manifest immediate results — sometimes it's hard to forgive what is perceived as a terrible transgression. If this is the case, then start forgiving the smaller issues first. Don't attempt to lift a forty-pound weight until you've worked your way up to it. And always remember to forgive yourself for not being able to forgive. If you sincerely want to release the past, you'll find a way to do it. It may take time and attention, but eventually you'll succeed. In the meantime, just do the best you can.

You can include enhancements in both sitting and walking meditations. The only difference in their execution is your body posture and choice of location. If you're walking, for example, you will need to keep your eyes open, or stop to lean against a tree for a few minutes. Just use common sense.

Step 4: Release

Release is the wrap-up portion of the whole sitting. You've given yourself a gift of time and purpose, and now you wrap it up like a present to be opened at your next practice. Release not only bridges the gap between meditative and everyday awareness levels, it also provides opportunity to deeply reinforce the entire encounter. This reinforcement makes your next sitting time easier to approach and more pleasant to experience.

Because meditative states in some ways resemble sleep without loss of awareness, returning to everyday consciousness takes a few minutes. Think of it as you do aerobic exercise. After you've completed your physical activity at a certain training level, you don't want to stop cold and sit down. You go through the cool-down period, giving your body a chance to gently return to its pre-exercise state. As with aerobics, when you've completed the "training" level of meditation (Centering), you then take a few minutes to gear up to non-meditative consciousness. This doesn't mean you leave the gifts of centering (objectivity, compassion, mindfulness) behind until your next session. The gifts do carry over into day-to-day living. But the extremely sensitive state of mind you generate during meditation shouldn't carry over — it's too intense.

Releasing is simple. Shift your consciousness from your breath (or from your current mental process) back to your body. Take a very deep breath and begin to move your fingers and toes. This reconnects you with your body. If you're walking, start to look around and pay closer attention to your surroundings. Next, acknowledge yourself for having allowed this experience to take place. Determine what was gained from the meditation. This is not a critical evaluation; it's an acknowledgment of the experience as laudable and constructive. You see, as a busy person, you'll tend to find a thousand reasons not to meditate regularly. If you devalue your efforts, you're not going to practice. It won't seem worth it. You're more likely to meditate regularly if you reinforce the positive aspects. I'm talking about an honest appraisal, respecting and acknowledging the gain from the experience, not parroting mundane cheerful statements that you don't really believe.

And what if the meditation seemed boring, frustrating, or otherwise low on the profit margin? If nothing else, the fact that you took time to do it demonstrates resolve and willingness. If you were distracted during the experience, then perhaps you practiced remaining compassionate and clear-headed in spite of your restless mental state. If your meditation was rewarding and uplifting, acknowledge that, too. If the experience isn't appreciated at some level, repeating it becomes a chore or an act of raw willpower that can only last so long.

Learning to meditate is a process much like learning to play the piano — the benefits are cumulative. The initial periods of piano practice can seem overwhelming and sometimes appear rote. But each time you sit down at the keyboard you wouldn't want to say to yourself, "Oh, I'm never going to learn to play the piano. I may as well give up." Instead you say, "Oh, I'm not such a great piano player right now and practicing scales is a little dull. But I can play a few simple tunes that I could never play before and I'm really excited about all the great music I'll soon be able to play. Not only that, but I'm exploring something I always wanted to do and that feels really good."

How Long Should You Meditate?

Ideally, meditation should be a daily practice, like brushing your teeth. Starting out the day from a place of centered calm makes for an infinitely more pleasurable and efficient life — not to mention the general self-esteem and sense of personal power that comes from having your own safe port in the storm. But because you're a busy person, asking for a daily practice of any discipline may be too much. If you can't find time for regular practice, then meditate whenever you can. The main point is to do it. Period. As you make meditation a priority, you'll find yourself carving out more and more time for it.

In a regular practice schedule, the following amount of time is recommended for beginners:

Step 1: Relax
Up to five minutes. Can be shorter as appropriate.

Step 2: Center
Start with five minutes, then increase as you feel the inclination.

Step 3: Enhance
Five to ten minutes.

Step 4: Release
One to five minutes.

As you can see, the base time here is about fifteen minutes. That's not a big chunk of time, even for a *very* busy person. But you may wonder about people who regularly meditate for at least thirty minutes, twice a day. They seem so committed. Is this fifteen minutes really good enough?

If fifteen minutes is all the time you can spare, then it's enough. Even thirty seconds of really clear awareness is well worth the time. Sure, it's great to take longer periods of silence when you can. But in any practice you have to start with where you are. If that means fifteen minutes is the most you can spare, then don't negate it. A few minutes of self-awareness without the usual litany of anger, judgment, and impossible standards is a major accomplishment in itself.

What if you can't spare fifteen minutes? This isn't at all uncommon among productive, involved people. Schedules get cramped, kids get sick, work piles up — the list of responsibilities is endless. Simply shorten each step and take only ten minutes.

Can't spare ten minutes? Then five minutes is okay. Can't spare five minutes? How about sixty seconds of serenity — using deep, focused breathing?

"Wait a minute," you say. "This can't be right, it's too lenient." Well, it may be lenient, but it leaves very little room for excuses. What counts is your intention to create even a single moment of conscious awareness in your daily schedule of responsibilities that cry for center stage. When you take even a moment to wake up from the somnambulance of everyday business, you begin to reclaim your right to *enjoy* life instead of *endure* it. At worst, these conscious moments give you perspective and help you remember that you are more than your current crisis. At best, these moments rekindle an appreciation of life's rich unpredictability, keeping you clearheaded, lighthearted, and open to new ideas. (Specifics on how to fit the MBP method into a very short time frame are described in Chapter 4, "Practical Use.")

Creating the Right Environment

Most people associate meditation with being alone in a quiet environment. The image of a deserted beach, desert wash, or mountaintop comes easily to mind — nice images and lovely places to sit, but not always available to a working person with family obligations. Are they really necessary? Not as long as you're breathing. Remember the breath? Your portable connection to mindfulness practice? Because you take your breathing everywhere, you can also meditate everywhere you take your breath. That means in the office restroom, at your desk, in a restaurant, on a walk, and yes, even alone in your room. A few minutes can be grabbed anywhere.

Requiring each meditation to occur in an undisturbed setting with incense and candles is a tall order. It also serves as a reasonable excuse not to attempt the practice at all. If you can turn within and focus on your breathing for even a few minutes, regardless of your location, you're practicing a form of meditation.

Do try for the undisturbed environment as a goal, but don't let environmental details interfere with your decision to practice. Any place will do. While you're waiting for a bus, focus on breath and become mindful of the moment. Commuting to work, focus on quiet breathing and simply be present to traffic without expectation. Brushing your daughter's hair, breathe with each downstroke and become aware of each strand of hair as you smooth it out.

Alone or with Company

If there are lots of people around, try to get some distance from them. You can relax for a moment in the nearest bathroom, go out to the car for a few minutes, or even stand by a window and gaze outside. Try to create some imaginary horizon. It might be helpful just to be honest and say, "I need a few minutes to gather my thoughts, okay?" Most people are more than willing to give you this time alone.

Getting distance from people doesn't necessarily apply if they want to join in the meditation. Meditation can also be a group activity when people get together for communal sittings. There is an inductive quality to group meditation that is very motivating. When others are sitting in silence around you, it's sometimes easier to become still. You're also more likely to stretch your "comfort zone" and add a few minutes to your meditation. Group practice is a welcome change provided you don't devalue your experience by comparing notes or becoming competitive about who sits the longest. (For more information on group meditation, see Chapter 3, "Staying Motivated.")

Pets

There are differing opinions on meditating in the presence of animals. If your pets are disruptive and you can get away from them, do so. If they pose no distraction or hazard, leave them alone. If you live in a suburban neighborhood you'll probably have to learn how to meditate through dogs barking, cats meowing, or kids yelling. Try allowing the noise to pass right through you; let it become just another sound in life's general hum.

Meditate with your animals present and absent. See which situation allows you to become centered and still with the least discomfort. It's usually easier to practice with cats; dogs can be more energetically demanding. You be the judge of what enhances and what distracts.

Music

Music is an incredible prop. It's a tool to spin your mind inward and open your heart. Music can move through your intellect with astounding ease, but it can also become an excessive distraction, twirling you in fantasy without any clear direction or control. Fine for daydreaming, but meditation is not the same as daydreaming.

The best kind of music is soft and gentle — noninvasive, a muffled backdrop in the meditation. If your music inspires rich feelings of joy or gratitude, add it during Step 3, the Enhancing portion of your practice. You don't want to distract yourself from the focal point during Step 2, Centering, but Step 3 has plenty of room for stimulating, vision-enhancing musical selections. If you want to delve into feelings of forgiveness, and you have a tape that sounds like a celestial choir, use it.

All kinds of music in various forms can be played during meditative processes, but as a general rule, the less distracting the music, the better. It's easy to get lost in music. If you do use music, keep an eye on prop dependency — using music as an excuse not to practice. ("I can't meditate without my favorite music.") Vary the music and its inclusion into the meditation as you would vary an exercise routine. After all, you may need to meditate for a shot of objectivity before some big presentation and your stereo won't be available then.

2

Beyond Getting Started

NOW THAT you've satisfied your initial how-to
curiosity, you can delve more deeply into other
aspects of meditating. In this chapter you'll learn how
to find the right meditation style, handle distractions,
and observe mental states before, during, and after
practice.

There's much more to meditating than just jump-
ing in and doing it — there's observation, refinement,

and infinite possibility. There's also much more to learn than is briefly covered here. When you're ready to explore the intricacies of meditation, you'll find many excellent books on the subject. (See Appendix 1 for a list of my favorites.)

About Meditation Styles

There are a number of meditation styles to choose from — almost as many as there are meditation teachers. But certain basic similarities shine through all of them. This section will loosely acquaint you with these similarities and help you realize what is available.

Similarities

Every form of meditation has an object of focus — something upon which to fix the mind. In some forms, the focal object is a repeated phrase or lyric (mantras and chants). In others, it's a visual focus such as a picture, or a flower, or even a part of the body. For still others, the focus may be physical movement such as rocking, dancing, or a martial art form. But the purpose of all focal points is the same: they teach you how to explore only one thought or image while diminishing the hold of other transient thoughts. This is a form of concentration that nurtures the development of mental agility, inner discipline, and greater awareness — handy qualities for maneuvering through a busy schedule.

For those meditators who want to merge with a deep devotional feeling or state of mind, the focal point may be the heart (representing loving kindness) or a beloved teacher such as Jesus or Buddha. The idea is to so identify with the focal point that devotion can transcend the image, and the meditator can then slip into a state beyond the ego. The meditator's goal is to merge into the consciousness that the focus represents — into loving, objective awareness.

For other meditators, the focal point is not selected for the purpose of merging with it, but rather for the purpose of emptying through it. The object may be the breathing cycle, or the forehead, or even the flow of thought. As the mind concentrates on one thing, other thoughts begin to drop away. Eventually, even the focal object disappears as the mind empties itself of all mental activity and rests in blissful nothingness, completely at peace. In this serene state of mind, meditators can open to the transitory nature of all words, thoughts, and actions. By experiencing the impermanence of life, they become insightful, objective, compassionate, and non-reactive.

So you see, it's basically either *merge with* or *empty through*. And often it may feel like you're doing one at one time and another at another time. The fact is, both processes have great import and usefulness. The ability to merge with profound heart energy provides inner strength in a world seemingly devoid of external support systems. The ability to empty your mind and accept impermanence is a necessary skill for living in a world where change is the only absolute. The MBP style combines both approaches.

Watching your breath without forcing it to do anything, and then dealing with your reactions by letting them pass is the emptying experience. As you watch your mind wind through a thousand different thoughts, you learn not to fight the flow, but rather to swim on top of it. You become graceful and more at ease with life's experiences. Because you understand life's ebb and flow, you don't grasp desperately at experiences or circumstances. You hold life lightly in your hands, giving yourself room to breathe and allowing a certain gentle humor and tolerance into your experience.

The MBP primary form (Steps 1, 2, and 4) fosters the development of your "witness" consciousness, a prerequisite for emptying your mind. The witness is the expansive, wise, objective part of you which sees the big picture. It observes the activity of your mind without being seduced by any single thought or feeling. And it delegates power and attention for the good of all of you, not just the satisfaction of individual urges. Like the physical body, your mind has many aspects to it — many functioning parts. Moods, beliefs, drives, and feelings each represent a limited portion of the totality of you. These aspects of mind make excellent followers but poor leaders and officers. The chief executive officer of your mind should be your witness consciousness. For example, if you see a cheesecake in the refrigerator, feelings of boredom or loneliness may whisper, "Who cares if we're not hungry. Let's eat it now." The witness may then note, "Ah, there's that old compulsive eating desire, loud as usual. But I know that once I've finished the snack, I'll still feel bad — maybe worse. Instead of eating, I'll do something more productive." When you engage your witness consciousness, you remain gently aware of your thoughts and feelings without drowning in them. In essence, you take better charge of your reactions and are no longer victimized by your own emotional riptides.

The MBP optional Enhancement (Step 3) replenishes your emotional spirit and offers the merging experience. Nourishing yourself with heart-directed visions, ideas, and feelings allows the childlike part of you to feel attended, safe, and courageous. After a rough day at the office or during times of stress and anxiety, reconnecting to the heart is an effective means of finding your own strength and comfort.

There is really no right or wrong way to meditate. Look at your own life and your own emotional state. Do you need to find self-love and be kind to yourself? Do you need to release the events of your day in compassion and objectivity? Meditation — any style of meditation — will make a difference in your life.

Finding the Right Style

Finding an appropriate meditation method is a process of trial and error. The selection of style involves shopping through books, classes and workshops, and satisfying your curiosity about which style seems easiest or most interesting. You need to allow yourself some healthy exploration to discover your preferences. It's a big world out there.

The first thing to do is to start with something — *anything*. Then do whatever you do as consistently as you can. As explained in Chapter 1, it's useful to begin with a method so you can then decide what you like and don't like about it. Practice one style regularly for a period of time (at least three months), to determine how it feels. Try not to style-hop every time you feel dissatisfied or restless. Those feelings are simply hindrances that show up in all forms of meditation sooner or later. They do not necessarily signal the need for change.

How do you know whether discomfort is present because you're dealing with natural resistance or because the meditation technique doesn't suit you? Take an honest look at your behavior. Self-seekers usually have a pretty good idea about their motivation for doing or not doing a practice. Does it feel like the same old resistance you meet every time you get uncomfortable with change? If so, maybe you need to sit with it for a while and investigate the distractions. See what they say to you. On the other hand, if you find yourself dreading practice time, the style may be a mismatch and you might need to shop around.

In either case, don't use your practice as an excuse for spiritual brutality — you know, "the no-pain-no-gain, if-I'm-miserable-it-must-be-good" school of enlightenment. Take it easy. If you'll stay open and aware — even on the edge of your comfort zone — you can learn from any style.

Work with different meditation styles as you are so inclined, but don't automatically assume that restlessness or boredom means you're doing something wrong. Eventually, you'll recognize certain mental states as old friends that pop up whenever you do your practice, regardless of the style you select.

Mental States Before Sitting

Let's get more specific. How should you approach your sitting? Well, just as an aircraft's approach to the runway greatly influences the ease of its landing, so your approach to your sitting affects the meditation. As you get close to practice time, you may experience a common form of resistance — the priority war. It happens to both beginning and experienced meditators. As soon as you decide to practice, a thousand priorities come to mind, all urgent.

Is my briefcase packed?

Did I turn off the coffee pot?

What am I going to do about retirement?

Should Antarctica be designated a world preserve?

Responsibility chaos. It tumbles through your mind at the mere suggestion of meditation.

When you really begin listening to your mind, you'll discover that much of your life is governed by fears, distractions, and a thousand "shoulds." These demanding taskmasters converge at meditation time to create a pandemonium of thought. In fact, Western culture actually supports this frantic pace of thinking and acting. The business world reinforces a schedule and mind crammed with appointments and activities. When you're extremely active and rushing through the day, it means you're responsible and "going for it."

Quietly observing your breath is contrary to the way your mind has been conditioned to operate; asking it to do something this subtle and unfamiliar tends to generate resistance. In this case, resistance takes the form of screaming voices of distraction.

What can you do? Simply observe the waterfall of thought. Watch one thought feed another and another. And when you've witnessed enough, you can coddle your nervous worries by saying, "It's okay. I'll only be sitting here for twenty minutes or so. In that time nothing disastrous is going to happen. I promise that when I'm done, if any of you are still around, I'll give you my full attention. Deal?" Even though they resemble dragons, these nervous worries and screaming priorities are actually more like insistent children. When you reassure them that meditation doesn't mean they won't receive their due regard, they tend to calm down and give you a little distance. Not much distance, mind you. Any one of these crying demands can be brought into full expression with your attention. But reassuring them and then telling them to go sit on a mental bench somewhere gives you room to move into quiet time. When you return from the silence, some of the concerns will come rushing back, but most won't — that is, until you get ready to meditate again.

Mental States During Sitting

Let's talk about the different mental states you may encounter during meditative practice. First we will discuss the generally pleasant mental states, and then we will cover denser feelings collectively grouped by the Buddhists into five categories: sloth, greed, restlessness, aversion, and doubt.

Buddhists consider all these mental states, pleasant and unpleasant, to be meditation hindrances. They are called hindrances because their expression can seduce your attention away from objective observance of the mind into the depth of feeling. You then become lost in fantasy, having moved from investigation to immersion.

Each of the mental states is inextricably linked with others. Feelings are tapestries of emotion. Disentangling their complexity helps you begin to see how depression usually follows elation, how anger wields the pleasure of power, how anxiety, boredom, and laziness generate and support one another. There really is no one mental condition that is devoid of the other states, nor does any one condition remain free from the tide of our emotional conditioning.

As you begin to witness the rise and fall of these mind states, you will see that it is your choice to indulge in them or to let them pass. You can then begin to experience your own mastery. You are no longer controlled by the breezy whims of a reactive mind. And the change comes not through time-honored willpower. Most busy people have enough willpower to boost a rocket. No. The change comes through wisdom and compassion for the human experience. This wisdom is cultivated through the Step 2 process, Centering, which helps you to remain focused in spite of your frailties and without harsh judgment of them. Composure and balance then emerge as you surrender to the vulnerability of being human.

Pleasant States

"This is incredible. Will I ever recapture it?"

Most meditators dream about the day when they will experience "Samadhi" — the indescribable rapture that sometimes occurs during meditation. Indeed, rapture is a wonderful goal and certainly a powerful motivator for regular practice. But what is it really like? Pleasant states of consciousness have an infinite variety of expression. You may feel gently calm and quiet, enjoying a respite from your usual waterfall of thought. You may feel physically light. You may experience sensations resembling small, delightful shocks of energy. And you may encounter none of the above — just an easy state of clarity and emotional freedom. Your adventure will be unique because your mind is unique.

These pleasant states are beguiling and rewarding, but they are not without their velvet traps. The traps lay not in the mind states themselves, but rather in your reactions to them. These wonderful feelings enchant and motivate, but they are by no means the end of the rainbow. For one thing, they can always get better, deeper, more peaceful, more profound. There is never a "best." And for another, pleasant states are not meant to deny the other aspects of your meditation. They are not better than, say, restlessness. Sure, they are more fun, more beautiful, and more motivating. (And as you become adept at quieting your mind, the pleasant states also become more common.) But there is no measure for spiritual worthiness that can rate one mind state as better than another. All have value. All offer wisdom.

The subtleties of pleasure will open as you surrender to them without comparison, judgment, or urgency. Pleasure becomes more than the obvious. Pleasure becomes part of the observation of other mind states — the pleasure of objectivity, the pleasure of freedom from reaction, the pleasure of change without resistance.

Here are a few ways to handle pleasant states:

1. When pleasure comes up, smile and welcome it with interest and care. Remember to breathe through the experience. Sometimes you can get caught in anticipation of the pleasant state's departure. You may begin to tighten your body in an unconscious effort that says, "If I don't move a muscle, then nothing will be disturbed and it won't go away." That response alone is enough to pull you into

a denser mental condition. If you can remain focused on your breath, your pleasurable event will be more likely to run its full, delightful course.

2. When you complete your meditation, write about the pleasure. Record the episode for future reference. As time passes, your doubting mind may try to devalue the experience. A written record will remind you that it really did happen and it really was special.

3. Sometimes pleasant states are as consuming as unpleasant states, and just like negative emotions, will pull you away from your centering focal point. If you lose sight of your primary object, your breath, then make the mental state your new primary object. Observe it as you would any mind state. Just watch as it ebbs and flows. Feel your tendency to grasp it as it ebbs. Observe the feelings that accompany the pleasure. Notice desperation trying to convince you to hold on to the experience, arguing that the

pleasant state may never return. (Of course, there's no need to worry. There's an abundance of pleasant states — more than you'll ever need.)

Sloth

"Hmmmm. That's a nice daydream. Maybe I'll take a little nap."

Sloth is apathy. Beyond ambivalence, it is inertia and presents itself as a sluggish, dull mind state. The mind begins to lose interest, but unlike boredom, it doesn't have the urgency to go on to something else. It just sits. Sloth and torpor lull the mind into wasteful daydreaming, slowly eroding any determination to practice.

Sloth is an attitudinal habit. It's an easy way to fool your mind into so little awareness that you don't even realize you're sinking into it. Sloth awakens just after your eyes are closed and your body is settled. You begin to sense that old familiar slide into careless attention and lethargy. Or sometimes it will mask itself as sleepiness, causing you to doze regardless of how much sleep you've already had.

When sloth approaches as drowsiness and loss of energy, simply take note of it. See sloth as separate from yourself. It is a condition that has draped itself over you; it is not you. Determine if the condition is appropriate. Are you really exhausted? Do you really need to take a nap? If so, decide to do it consciously and then snooze away. If not, here are a few ways to handle sloth:

1. *Check your body posture.*

Are you sitting up straight? Is your head sinking into your neck or lifting up from it? As a general rule, your body posture is a good indicator of the presence of sloth even before it becomes a problem. Keep your body steadily generating energy. If your body is putting forth some serene effort to maintain poise, it is generally enough energy to keep you attentive and awake. If you're plagued with drowsiness, try to avoid meditating while lying down or in bed. Lying down is a trigger for sleep and it can be a set-up for sloth. Consider doing some walking meditations to generate more energy, or if you have to lie down to meditate, do it in a room where you don't ordinarily sleep.

2. *Check your scheduled practice time.*

Are you meditating when you're already exhausted? Try meditating at a different time of the day or in different circumstances. Although sittings are the perfect pick-me-up after a long hard day, if you're falling into la-la land, you need to rekindle the memory of energy and do it at a time that supports that goal.

3. *If the sloth is too difficult to ignore, make it your focal point.*

Examine it with interest. Generate your own energy separate from the drain of inertia. Watch the thoughts that come up with a lazy mind. What precedes the sloth? What happens when you simply attend to the tiredness as a primary focus? Is it then replaced with frustration or anger? Watch it slide into your consciousness over well-worn paths and settle in with confidence. Observe its reaction when you sit along side it, objective and attentive to its next move. Does it shrug its shoulders and drift away? Does it take root and stubbornly refuse to leave?

4. If all else fails, shorten the duration of your meditations.

Maybe you're trying too much at once and the resistance is telling you something about your expectations. Remember, meditation is a skill. Give yourself time to learn how to tolerate longer periods of quiet. Try shortening your practice time in order to create the feeling of a refreshing, energetic experience.

Greed

"I'm doing this meditation to experience cosmic consciousness and I want it *now.*"

In meditation, greed displays itself through an obsessive lust for results. Because greed is often confused with earnest desire, it's important to distinguish between the two. Greed stems from fear and lack. It fuels competition, pitting each meditation against the next, each meditator against the other. Greed says that there is only so much available so you had better get your share before anybody else does. Greed devalues any experience leaving you deflated, depressed, and frustrated.

On the other hand, healthy desire emanates from the heart, intuitively fed by positive expectancy. It approaches each experience as a building block, open to the unexpected pleasures that await and compassionate toward any struggles that may ensue. The pleasure of growth and achievement is constant when you are centered in healthy desire. Your forward momentum comes not from grasping, but from natural creative expansion.

The distinction between greediness and healthy desire is subtle. If you can't distinguish between them, try observing the ebb and flow of your behavior. Greed flows as grasping fear, urgency, and desperation. When it ebbs, it leaves a wake of bitterness, frustration, and insecurity. Healthy desire flows as creative expression, expansiveness, and hopefulness. When healthy desire ebbs into dormancy, it's like the still of winter: creative, but in repose like a resting cat.

Because greed can be so consuming, when you see it you may become frightened and try to push it away. Don't be concerned, however, the emotion of greed is natural, and will pass, like everything else. It's just a childlike part of you that wants everything and thinks it never has enough. It comes and goes in various forms throughout life. Watch for it and be open to its lessons. Greed can tell you a lot about how hard you are on yourself, how frightened you are, or how lonely you've become. It's a powerful signal to look deeper within.

As you begin to see greed in your practice, you may also notice greed in your daily affairs. Sometimes, it may seem like greed is your only motivating force. Again, don't be hard on yourself or hate the greediness you observe. Even though greed is never satisfied, the momentum it creates can result in many wonderful accomplishments.

Here are a few ways to handle greed:

1. *Face it openly and honestly.*

Observe your feelings. One moment you're okay with current circumstances, the next you're agonizing over them. That's the edge of greed. Don't become upset. Just remain observant. Meet greed and its attendants with compassion. Watch its urgency and fear. Note the desperation and say, "There's greed. Isn't that interesting. Oh, look what greed is trying to tell me."

2. *Try welcoming it.*

When you see greed rising to the surface, embrace it as an old compatriot. Say "Hi there! We've come a long way together. Have a cup of coffee and we'll talk a while." This isn't as silly as it sounds. If you approach rejected aspects of yourself with regard and appreciation, you become open to their value and can reap their rewards without indulging in them. This kind of objectivity leaves you clear, vitalized, and ready for transformation.

Restlessness

"Why can't I relax? Why won't my mind calm down?"

Restlessness is a common and frustrating meditation hindrance that appears as physical discomfort, twitching muscles, or an "antsy" feeling. It can also be a mental discomfort such as anxiety, general nervousness, or worry. Restlessness frequently shows up when you are getting close to making a change. The challenge to remain still may seem unbearable at times, but remember that restlessness can appear more demanding than it really is.

Here are a few ways to handle restlessness:

1. Note the restlessness, whatever its form, and return to your breath over and over again. This is the basic Step 2, Centering, procedure. Just keep working with it.

2. Try changing your body posture. For example, shift from sitting to walking. Walking gives your muscles something to do and your mind something tangible to grasp. It also gives you an opportunity to reconnect with the pleasure of your quiet time. But don't use walking as an excuse not to sit. Keep working with your sitting posture.

3. Make the physical feeling of restlessness your focal point. Instead of trying to ignore it, look directly at it. Observe restlessness in your body. One sensation after another fades in and out, blending into an overall experience of physical or mental confusion. When you can sort out the responses and

follow them individually, you'll be able to step back from their urgency. The feelings may then diminish, like the tingling sensations of a leg that's waking up.

4. If your restlessness appears as worry and anxiety, make the worrisome thoughts your focal point. Observe how one concern stimulates another and another. Investigate the tumbling feelings. Separate from the experience by saying, "Oh there's nervousness. And there it is again. Isn't that interesting." Rather than rejecting the images, have compassion for yourself for feeling them. Quietly make room for their desperation, allowing them to pass in front of your mind like slides on a screen.

Aversion

"This is tedious and dull. Maybe I need a new style." "I'll never be able to quiet my mind. It's hopeless."

Aversion simply refers to rejection. In meditation, rejection cloaks itself in many forms, the most common being boredom and despair. Underneath each of these feelings is fear, the basis of all aversion. In meditation, it's usually fear of change — a powerful block to growth. You see, any change in your approach to living has ramifications that can scare you. For example, taking responsibility for certain aspects of your life may require giving up favorite avoidance behaviors such as self-pity. Or if you're steeped in depression, you may have to take some action. Changing any kind of ingrained response usually brings up fear, so your ego may hide in aversion to avoid facing these concerns. Aversion helps maintain the status quo — keeping it close and familiar no matter how uncomfortable it may be.

Boredom is probably one of the most familiar forms of aversion. Busy people whose lives are filled with continual stimulation are especially prone to boredom. Without a barrage of external stimuli, your mind will at first consider the resulting quiet to be boring. ("Nothing's happening. I need to do something else.") Boredom makes the mind drift, longing for any distraction. Boredom tries to convince you that your meditation isn't interesting or appropriate. It rejects whatever you're doing. If boredom can't convince you to give up meditating entirely, it will convince you to switch meditation styles.

Despair is another common form of aversion. Despair gives up without a fight and takes the easy way out. ("I'll never be able to do this. Why bother?") Despair, like greed, devalues the current experience, whatever it is, seeking only the perfection of unrealistic expectations. It seduces you with promises of relief from the struggle, and after you've given in, it pounds you with inadequacy and remorse.

Here are a few ways to handle aversion:

1. With boredom, note its frantic handwaving and return to your breath. Boredom is a mesh of

feelings that mostly reject you and your experience. If the boredom is consuming, then make it your focal point. Underneath boredom is the fear that nothing will ever happen and, of course, that the style of meditation you have selected is totally wrong for you.

With despair, examine its draining pull. If you give in to the anguish and stop meditating, watch guilt and judgment step in. Observe how these feelings leap-frog through your consciousness, keeping you in turmoil and self-condemnation. Make despair your focal point, and persist without fueling destructive, failure-promoting habits of thought. Simply watch these thoughts and sit right alongside them without absorbing their energy or acting on them.

2. If boredom has been nagging you for some time, try a slight change in format such as walking, adding music on occasion, meditating with other people, or meditating outdoors. Read Chapter 3,

"Staying Motivated," and try a few of those suggestions. But don't be afraid to experiment with boredom. Allow for the occasional desire to try new ideas, look deeply inside yourself and ask, "Am I just exploring meditation in another way, or am I really avoiding the process and looking for reasons to eventually quit?" Be honest with yourself. Just because you add a little music to your sitting doesn't mean you've given in to the hindrance or that your practice is doomed.

If despair is hanging around, use your intellect to convince yourself to continue practicing. You've probably experienced despair in other areas of your life. Has giving up in despair ever solved a problem? Find a meditation group or talk with a meditation teacher. Get a sense of what is really going on with your despair. Perhaps you have unearthed some deep, habitual responses and now have the opportunity to gently move through them using your practice as a guide. If so, congratulations.

Doubt

"Why am I wasting my time with this? Maybe I'm just crazy." Doubt is an intellectual tool designed to help think through opinions, reconsider decisions, and identify fallacies. It's useful when it sparks healthy activity and real investigation. But if it sticks to you without prompting further action, devalues your intuition, and creates a spiral of self-condemnation, then it's a hindrance.

In meditation, doubt can be insidious. It sneaks up through other hindrances. If you're bored, doubt slips in and questions your reasoning. If you're sleepy, doubt says that this is a bad time of day. If you're restless, doubt says you aren't cut out for meditation. Doubt is slippery because it masquerades as reasonable behavior. Although the proof of meditation is in the practice, doubt will cause you to stop believing in the positive results and set you up for despair. ("Why am I doing this? I'm not really changing. I must be an idiot to think this will improve my life.")

Here are a few ways to handle doubt:

1. Go to a class, find a book, or talk to another meditator. Probably the best way to dispel doubt is by talking to an expert or associating with people of like mind. Remind yourself of the reasons you initially began this study. Remind yourself of the benefits you've already experienced and the good things yet to come. Then test your reality with people you respect. They'll tell you you're not crazy.

2. Keep a practice diary or a journal. When doubt questions your commitment or results, you can look through your journal and read the results aloud to yourself. There they are, in black and white. The journal provides you with snapshots of your success.

3. Doubt the doubt. Use it as a response to itself. When doubt comes in, look for other hindrances. Is it here because you feel discouraged

(aversion)? Are you doubting because you talked to someone whose meditation experiences are more transcendental than yours (greed)? Are you bored and looking for an excuse to quit (aversion)? Are you daydreaming a lot (sloth)? Look beneath the doubt and see if there is another hindrance creating or supporting it. Then attend to *that* problem.

4. Observe the doubt and make it your focal point. Say to yourself, "Oh, there's doubt again. What does it want me to do now? Hmmmm." Then watch it transform into anger, then depression, then anxiety, then sleepiness, or whatever. Be attentive to the changes without judgment. Gently observe them.

Mental States After Sitting

When your sitting is completed, there is the after-sitting frame of mind. As with the sitting itself, the after-sitting state can vary quite a bit. If the meditation was particularly deep, you may feel a little "spacey" and ungrounded. That's fine. At times you may feel peaceful and soft, like something important has happened. Other times you'll immediately feel razor sharp and ready for action. Empowered. Awakened. Stimulated. Still other times you'll feel the same as you did before meditating. But again, one thing is certain: the benefits of meditation are cumulative. The more you do it, the better you generally feel.

You might think of your practice as you would think of planting a seed. It's not something that you watch every second to see if you're getting somewhere. If you keep digging up a seed to see if anything is happening, it simply won't grow. Even if you leave it alone, but keep looking at it every fifteen minutes, you won't see measurable change. The seed grows gradually, but surely. It starts its growth not by shooting into the sky, but rather by sending roots into the earth. It grows deeper before it is seen above ground. And when it finally appears, the change is noticeable and satisfying to view. With meditation, you need to trust that positive change is happening. Regardless of your mental state, know that you are sending roots into the soil of your consciousness, and soon the benefits will be obvious.

Most beginning meditators go through the ex-smoker syndrome, that is, the familiar self-righteous attitude that says, "I'm doing this so you should, too." It seems to be the nature of people to trumpet a good thing. Right after a nice long sitting you may feel particularly motivated to share the wealth with your family and friends. It's tempting to tell everyone how much they can gain from this practice. Of course, they do have much to gain, but they're unlikely to be interested if you hound them about it.

The best way to encourage your friends to meditate is to mention that you do it, then don't say another word. If you meditate regularly, your friends will notice the change. And when they notice, they'll ask more than idle questions. This is your opportunity to tell them about the benefits of sitting. But if you tell them before they ask, they're likely to respond with, "Oh, that's nice," and go on their merry way, ignoring your noble intentions and life-changing message. As with any healthy, enlightened practice such as reading, meditation, or exercise, your own life is your best advertisement.

3

Staying Motivated

I T'S ONE THING to get started in your meditation practice, but it's another thing to keep going with it. If you are a person who starts fast but fizzles in the stretch, this chapter is for you. It's designed to help you stay with your practice even when your enthusiasm wanes and your patience runs low. You'll learn three main requirements for keeping motivation high, and discover how to regenerate eroding enthusiasm through the use of props, schedules, groups, and teachers.

Motivation Requirements

The ability to spark the fire of enthusiasm after it has smoldered is a skill anyone can develop. To start a practice, you must have a strong initial desire and enthusiasm — qualities well represented in our culture. But to continue the practice you must be flexible and persistent. The trick is first, to accept that the flush of start-up excitement won't last, and second, to realize that waning interest is something that comes and goes with any endeavor. Just because your enthusiasm isn't hot and burning doesn't mean the practice has lost its value to you.

There are three requirements for maintaining your motivation:

1. *Allow for Mistakes*

Cultivate a willingness to allow human failing in your meditations. It's difficult to continue a practice if you constantly berate yourself. ("I blew it again! Why can't I stay focused? What is my problem?")

Allow yourself to be imperfect, inconsistent, distracted — in a word, "human." Think of your mind as an undisciplined puppy. When you teach a puppy to focus on one behavior, such as sitting or staying, you expect it to take time to adapt to your request. First the puppy has to understand what you mean, then it has to realize that you mean it when you say it, and finally it has to become so comfortable with the new behavior that it replaces its old habits of running around and ignoring you. Each of these training steps takes time and diligence.

The metaphor is obvious. You've spent years without paying much attention to your thoughts. And having television as a major stimulus, your mind is accustomed to short periods of concentration on powerful images. Give yourself time to adapt — the subtleties of meditation can take some time to integrate.

2. *Don't Give Up Too Soon*
Be willing to work through the "wall of resistance." This wall is thick with procrastination,

perfectionism, and doubt. It can show up at any time, diffusing your energy and interfering with your practice. Because it seems so formidable, the natural inclination is to push hard — to knock it down, to hate it.

Unfortunately, this wall won't stay down no matter how hard you push. You see, as long as you are human, you'll be dealing with resistance at some level. It's called human nature, and hating it doesn't change it. Accepting that there are going to be times when the wall shows up, helps to quell the surge of frustration and its eventual result: despair.

When you see the wall, acknowledge it as a passing state and continue to meditate. Engage in gentle persistence instead of reacting in anger, desperation, or frustration. These feelings take you out of the moment and leave you depleted and exasperated. The wall will come up now and then regardless of how experienced you are or how balanced you think you've become. If you struggle against it, soon you won't want to practice anymore because you'll be so tired of the conflict. So, rather than fight, see the wall as an old acquaintance and continue with your practice. Remove the drama from the battle and say to yourself, "Ah, there are my old feelings of distraction and anxiety. We've been together before. Now back to breath." Gentle persistence is the key.

3. *Remember Why You're Doing It*

Reconnect with the intuitive knowing that says meditation can make your life better. This deep sense doesn't always manifest as strong attraction; sometimes it feels like a constant, low-grade pull. You may hear about meditation and wonder about it. You may meet people whom you respect and then discover they meditate. You may see articles about meditation in the newspaper. It keeps tugging on you. Whatever form the attraction takes, pay attention. It's a personal signal. Remind yourself of the allure. Read books that refresh your memory and motivate you.

The above three requirements needn't all be fully in place when you begin your practice. They can be cultivated just like other mental capacities. But be aware of their opposites: perfectionism, impatience, and inflexibility. When you recognize one of these emotional states, step outside yourself and say something like, "Well, there's old inflexibility again. Guess it's reminding me to give myself a break." Instead of chafing at dense emotional states that come up from time to time, use them as reminders to keep you on track. When you can see the denser states as only part of your nature — certainly not all of it — you can begin to feel less trapped by them. Simple awareness lets you know you have a choice. And the more you consciously choose the lighter emotional states, the better you will be at remaining in them.

Remember that lack of motivation can be observed just like any other mind state. You can actually witness your excuses. Feel their urgency, their groundless fears, their fancy footwork. Note them with compassion, but don't try to figure them out. Figuring is another intellectual mind state — something you don't need to develop any further. Just observe. Watch the rising and the subsequent falling of your mind state. As soon as you recognize the changeable nature of your mind, you won't become hooked by dense, negative feelings or hindrances. You'll be better able to acknowledge their seduction, knowing that they, too, shall pass.

Now that we've talked a little about motivation and resistance, let's look at a few props to assist you during times of low enthusiasm. Although you don't want to become superstitious about using specific items, being in special rooms, or wearing certain clothing, you can still explore various meditation props as part of your experiential research. You might even try creating your own simple ceremony as a way of personalizing your practice.

Using Props

Items such as incense, robes, candles, pictures, religious symbols, and music can all be considered props. These props are fun and very motivating. They keep interest levels high and may even assist in achieving states of deep quiet. Props create an ambiance that makes you feel warm and good about your practice. Their only drawbacks are that they aren't generally portable and it's easy to become dependent on them. Use them with care. You can't wear a meditation robe in a typical business meeting. You can't depend on a candle as a centering object while standing in line at a busy airport. Attachment to a favorite item is bound to occur, but remember that your power is not in outside objects, conditions, or circumstances. Your power is inside of you. So guard against becoming superstitious. Objects only have as much power as you give them.

Clothing

The ritual of changing from one form of clothing to another can have great impact on one's state of mind. We tend to imbue clothes with a lot of meaning.

Party clothes feel festive. Pajamas make us sleepy. Business suits are powerful. So why not use clothing to make us feel like meditating?

Meditation garments feel nice. When you take off your workday clothes and don your special robe, a settled feeling and a sense of safety take over. Some people describe this phenomenon as removing confused and anxious energy patterns of the day and slipping into quiet, gentle energy patterns of meditation.

If you have a flair for the dramatic and you're having trouble keeping up with sittings, try creating a loose robe to support you in the transition from work to practice. Or designate a favorite sweatsuit as your meditation attire. If you do change into a robe or some special garment before practicing, notice how it affects your mind state, turning the transition from work to quiet time into a kind of gracious ritual. But regardless of your clothing choice, beware of becoming attached to it. Since clothes don't meditate for you, don't give them too much power.

Objects and Items

Items such as incense, bells, or pictures can serve several purposes in your practice. They can be primary focal objects, symbolic reminders of your spirituality, or tools to use in conjunction with various mental processes.

1. *Primary Focal Objects*

Anything can be a primary focal object (see Chapter 1), but some items are more emotionally satisfying than others. A candle, for example, is a much more interesting focal point than a glass of water, yet either is an adequate device for centering. Remember that a focal object provides your mind with something upon which to fix its attention. Benignly observing an object (like a candle) or a process (like breathing) can help to steady the wild mind. It also helps you to concentrate more efficiently and to flow with conditions in a nonjudgmental way.

2. *Symbolic Reminders*

Such things as crystals, wands, incense, and symbols of faith such as crosses, statues, rosaries, or even censers can all symbolize various spiritual qualities or states of consciousness. Symbolic reminders are as diverse as primary objects. Some people believe that certain items become energetically connected to practice time and, therefore, are very valuable. Holy objects have been passed down from generation to generation in families, churches, and spiritual orders. Symbols can penetrate the intellect and move right to the heart. They stimulate feelings and touch us at very deep levels.

3. *Tools*

Tools used for mental processes include meditation and musical tapes, pictures, lists, photographs, books, or whatever items help trigger your perceptions and enhance your experience. For example, in forgiveness work it is sometimes helpful to view pictures of loving saints, spiritual teachers, or devoted friends. Pictures of kind souls can inspire compassion, stimulate vision, and help you see situations from a new, less rigid, perspective. The MBP method supports the use of tools during optional Step 3, Enhancement.

Use any prop that helps you feel centered and aware — something that pulls you into your core. The only catch is not to give it so much importance that you feel lost or powerless without it. Stay in touch with the true source of power — your own spirit. Props may serve to trigger deep personal feelings, but they should not be requirements for making this connection. This ability is always present even though you usually don't pay attention to it.

Meditation props may be stored in drawers or closets to protect them from prying eyes, but it's also nice to display them. Designate a display table or shelf near your meditation chair or pillow. Group the pictures, beads, censers, or whatever you have chosen into a pleasing arrangement on the table. Looking at all your spiritually "charged" items can signal your mind that it's time to go within and make practice time more personally fulfilling.

Creating Your Own Ritual

Rituals communicate at a very deep level. They are used to comfort, to stir, to join, and to release. There's nothing mysterious about rituals or ceremonies. They don't have to be religious; they can be family oriented, professional, even recreational. A ritual simply prepares the mind and body for what comes next. For example, if you usually set the table before dinner, the ritual of placing dishes in an eating arrangement can trigger the mind and body to expect to eat. Finishing dinner and putting your fork down can then stimulate an expectation for after-dinner coffee. Everyday rituals like these are common within all cultures.

A ritual can be very helpful when you're trying to calm down and tune in. A simple ceremony of changing from street clothes to loose meditation attire can create the mood to meditate. Or, before practice you may stretch your neck and legs, light a subtle incense, and then read a page or two from a favorite book. The stretching helps to relax your body, the incense is a powerful sensory signal, and the reading helps to quiet your mind and perhaps inspire you.

If you usually meditate in a certain body posture, this posture then becomes a physical reminder of what you are about to do — a physical observance. Certain hand positions, such as palms turned upward in your lap, can also prepare your mind for practice. The palms-upward position suggests surrender, vulnerability, openness. These mental conditions free you from rigid preconceptions, cultivating a state known as "beginner's mind." They help you step back from careening thoughts, allowing you to center with greater ease.

Another aspect of your meditation ceremony is the time of day when you sit. Even though the MBP concept encourages you to meditate whenever you can, you may at some point decide to make meditation an everyday practice. When you do, try to meditate at the same time each day. As the time of day reminds you to eat and sleep, so the time of day can initiate you into quiet. The body knows what's coming and can start to calm itself and move into meditation mode. Further, when you've designated a particular time as your meditation break, it's no longer subject to debate. You don't waste time worrying, "Should I do it now, or later?" You have one less decision to make and one less opportunity to procrastinate.

Scheduling Your Practice

If you're like most busy people, the last thing you need is another item to schedule. You hate scheduling. Scheduling leaves no room for spontaneity. It sets you up for failure, and gives you another reason to feel frustrated and ineffective. You might even think there's no way you can schedule one more thing because your life is already so crazy.

Well, guess what? Scheduling, when done properly, works. And it doesn't have to rob you of spontaneity, set you up for failure, or drive you crazy.

Most of your personal time is grounded in habit. You habitually undertake certain activities and avoid others. Following habit is like taking a familiar path — it's a lot easier to walk down a well-trampled footpath than to bushwhack another one. But when you want to add a new activity to your routine, you have to blaze a new trail. It takes extra energy to do this, but there are tools that can make your work go much faster and easier.

Your schedule is a tool designed to assist you in doing what you really want to do. It helps you tread a new routine and truly is your friend. But if you view your schedule as a punitive parent which you must yield to and satisfy, of course you're going to rebel. Yet who turned it into a parent? You did.

How does this relate to meditation? Simple. You're a busy person. You need something to help you claim that extra half-hour and assign it specific value and purpose. You need to prevent time from running through your hands like sand. Result: a schedule.

To be effective, your schedule must be visible, legible, and malleable. You don't need to write everything down, nor should you. List only the events you need to specifically address — in this case, your meditation time. Leave the rest blank. If you try to plan too much, you'll become overwhelmed. Keep the schedule as uncomplicated as possible and post it where you can easily see it. If something comes up and you can't make your practice time, don't throw your hands up screaming, "Schedules don't work!" Just try your schedule for the rest of the week and then reevaluate it. If it doesn't work, change it.

The point is that a schedule can be a valuable tool, helping you accomplish things you really *want* to do but have *resistance* to doing. It can also help you establish a new pattern of behavior or get through a particularly busy time. And too, scheduling frees your mind to concentrate on what is at hand. This is known as efficiency — something busy people really like.

Working with Groups, Teachers, Retreats

A particularly enjoyable way to keep motivation high is by associating with other meditators. This can be done by participating in a meditation group, obtaining counsel from a teacher, or periodically going on retreat.

Groups

One of the best ways to stay motivated is to connect with a group of like-minded individuals. Contrary to appearances, meditation is not necessarily a solitary activity. In fact, it's beneficial to regularly meditate with a group. Groups are inspirational. It's stimulating to see other people value this practice as much as you do, and it also helps to know that other people are going through the same things you are. Further, there is an inductive quality to group meditation that can actually deepen your practice. Groups provide an energetic support that creates special meditative experiences.

The only potential drawback to meditating with a group is the human tendency to compare notes. A good rule-of-thumb is not to discuss the details of your meditations with other people. It leads to comparisons, judgments, and inner dialogue like, "Why can't I meditate for forty-five minutes like Sarah over there?" or "John has transcendental experiences every time he closes his eyes and I never do. Maybe I'm wasting my time." Although our rational mind measures its progress on an emotional worthiness scale (distraction is bad; exaltation is good), in the stillness of meditation we have a unique opportunity to appreciate all emotional levels — from despair to serenity. Each level has value. Each level holds wisdom.

Unfortunately, our culture invites competition and it's almost inconceivable not to compare and contrast results. But if these comparisons occur, simply note them. They are a natural response and needn't become a problem unless you use them to batter yourself.

Remember, your meditation practice isn't a contest against other meditators. Although there are basic meditation models to follow, everybody has a different set of issues to confront. Expecting yourself to have experiences identical to someone else is unrealistic. Meditation is an adventure in consciousness — not somebody else's consciousness, but yours alone. Your experiences will reflect your unique character.

Still, the inevitable questions and concerns may arise. And when these questions can't be resolved by discussion with a friend, you may decide to look for a good meditation teacher.

Teachers

Finding a good meditation teacher sometimes involves a little research. Meditation teachers usually counsel in several disciplines, meditation being one of them. If you have a local New Age periodical, you can peruse the classes and seminars offered. You might also attend a few church services and ask around. If you keep your eyes and ears open, you'll find someone to help you along.

When you're in the beginning stages of practice, it's hard to know which teacher is most appropriate. Some teachers travel a great deal, offering you only occasional opportunities to hear them speak. Buddhist monks sometimes travel and teach in this manner. Other teachers will host regular group meditations and schedule private sessions whenever you choose.

Teacher accessibility isn't the only variable guiding your selection; another big factor is meditation style. Some teachers work with music or chanting, some instruct only the Centering practice (sometimes known as Vipassana or insight meditation), and others include more direct philosophical instruction. It's natural to feel a little overwhelmed by the alternatives available. Like most meditation students, you may end up trying out several teachers. But if you practice all four steps of the MBP method, you won't be totally unprepared for the diversity. The MBP steps provide a strong foundation for the variety of concentration techniques you may encounter. After some healthy exploration, you'll begin to get a sense of the kind of teacher most appropriate to your skill and interest levels.

Generally speaking, meditation teachers should be compassionate, inspirational, well-practiced in their chosen arena, and aware of their own shortcomings. Although these qualities sound almost saintly, you must remember that teachers are human beings. They may practice longer, express themselves better, or exude a certain mastery, but they are still people with egos to integrate, personal preferences, and growth issues to confront. Honor them for their wisdom, but don't invest them with godlike qualities. What they can do, you can do. (With more experience, you could be a teacher as well.) The point is that the more you separate yourself from them, the less of their teaching and qualities you can absorb. Devotion to a teacher is a powerful means of learning, but it must be tempered with an objective, reasoning mind. Stay clearheaded, and resist the temptation to worship your teacher. Good teachers don't want to be worshipped — they just want to teach. There are no rules here except to remain ethical, balanced, and true to your own sense of morality.

Retreats

Meditation retreats can have a profound impact on your practice, or they can just provide good companionship and interesting experiences. It depends on the kind of retreat you are considering. Some retreats are more social than others; you may discover one that is as much an encounter group as it is a meditation experience. Other retreats are completely unstructured, allowing you to do whatever you want to do and meditate whenever you like. Still others are much more intense, providing organized periods of meditation processes alternating with walking, sitting, eating, and resting.

If you are interested in a retreat or workshop, call the organizers and ask if they cater to beginning meditators. Some retreats are specifically geared to beginners; others require a certain amount of practice background. Don't be afraid to ask questions. Make sure you are comfortable with the demands that will be placed on you. Discuss the food and sleeping accommodations; some retreats are more rugged than others. Ask about the practice schedules. If the shortest meditation sitting is one hour and you've never spent more than twenty minutes in silence, you may have some difficulty.

Going on a meditation retreat requires a little bravery. The busy mind gets nervous at the concept of meditating for more than a few stolen minutes. But the physical, psychological, and spiritual results are well worth the effort. Physically, retreats are very refreshing. They usually take place in a pleasant setting with room to stretch, relax, and reconnect to your body. Psychologically, retreats provide a wonderful break from your work routine and strengthen your confidence as a meditator. You may overcome your fear of meditating for longer periods of time, or feel stronger about your practice and vitalized in your commitment to it. Spiritually, retreats are nourishing at a deep soul level, pulling you out of a sense of powerlessness which is common in our Western culture. You'll feel refreshed not only by the practices themselves, but also from associating with other participants. Meditators can renew your faith in human nature since they are generally a nice, aware, sincere group of people.

If you're feeling anxious about a retreat, but still want to go, then make sure you have permission to take a walk or to leave at your discretion. You probably won't need to get away, but it helps to know the option is available. Even if requirements seem rigorous, don't write them off as impossible. Being in a retreat setting can foster great leaps in capacity. You may surprise yourself, returning home with a greatly expanded view of meditation and your involvement with it.

4

Practical Use

WHAT IS the meditation question most often asked by busy people? It isn't about mechanics or technique. Nor does it involve the mental states of boredom or bliss. The question most often asked is this: "What is the practical value of meditating?" In other words, how can you apply the benefits of meditation to everyday circumstances?

Because the benefits of meditation, such as balance and objectivity, are somewhat intangible, this chapter offers suggestions on the functional application of meditation and its cumulative rewards. In these pages you can begin to see how your new practice affects your life in a general sense and how you can apply specific aspects of meditation to everyday events. This information should not only help you weather frustrating circumstances, but also motivate you to keep practicing. Finally, there is a section at the end of the chapter that addresses positive expectancy and its relationship to meditation.

General Practicality

Meditation is practical as both a general discipline and a balancing tool. As a general discipline, it deepens conscious awareness of your unique talents and capabilities. Your self-confidence grows to allow more room to take risks, to enjoy living, and to manage stress. As a balancing tool, it helps you maintain an objective clarity, supporting you in circumstances that may otherwise throw you emotionally off-center.

Meditation helps you learn how to rest and savor the moment without interfering with your forward momentum. To savor the moment is to create a momentary break between forward steps. In mountain hiking, for example, there is a gait that calls for a brief pause after each step forward, allowing you to catch your breath. When you employ this gait and take advantage of the break, you are able to scale incredible heights without wasting energy or attention and go farther than you ever thought possible. That's what meditation does. It helps you to catch the moment and breathe deeply through it, replenishing your energy, increasing your endurance, and expanding your horizons.

Objectivity

Busy people are creative, determined folks who sometimes miss life's pleasures because of burdensome responsibilities. The ups and downs of daily commitments keep their minds so cluttered that there is little room for simple receptivity. Regular meditation won't dissolve the clutter, but it will increase the capacity to move through it with steady ease. This steadiness develops by learning to observe life without judgment — by practicing an attitude of objectivity. You see, we tend to take most experiences far too personally. We get caught up in externally produced chaos and then react as if it is our personal problem and responsibility. When this happens, our judgment clouds and we slip into old destructive patterns of behavior that keep us feeling frustrated, trapped, and emotionally confused.

Using objectivity, we begin to see through the confusion and realize that even though we may not be able to change external events, we can surely change our reactions to them. This puts us firmly on the path of resolution — a path that can lead to several positive conclusions. We may discover a new, more effective way to handle the situation; we may change our attitudes so that the situation is no longer bothersome; we may even be able to change the situation itself. Let's look at two simple examples.

The freeway rush-hour commute is a familiar example of personalizing an external event. Especially when you're late for work, you can easily become anxious and indignant with sluggish traffic. If a driver cuts in front of you, you may begin to make reckless driving decisions to even the score. Every other driver represents competition for speed and space. Intellectually, you know the freeway isn't a private battleground, but emotionally, it's hard not to take personal offense. And why shouldn't you? In an age when most people feel powerless as individuals, anger can resurrect a brief, dynamic memory of personal authority. Primal feelings are commanding, and anger makes you feel mighty. Add to these feelings a symbolic weapon of control like a car, and you have a unique opportunity to act out with vehemence. Although there's nothing inherently wrong with wanting to feel powerful, acting powerful with a weapon makes it potentially dangerous. And the real question is, do you really want to get this upset over something as mindless as a traffic jam?

The drama of an angry reaction wears deep paths in the subconscious mind and can become habitual. But objectivity will help. You've been practicing objective observance of your breath during Step 2, Centering, and now you can begin to exercise those techniques in new arenas. Right there in the middle of a traffic jam, you observe your habitual behavior as it begins its morning display. You begin to see the false sense of satisfaction it supports. You begin to understand that the feelings of power you receive from this display are hollow and temporary.

Observing all aspects of your behavior, both constructive and nonconstructive, places you in a mode of choice. Instead of becoming a victim of traffic chaos, you're just a person in heavy traffic. You can decide whether battling the interstate is worth the safety risk as well as the expenditure of energy and attention. This objectivity places you consciously at the helm of your decisions, and frees you from the tyranny of reaction.

Another example of taking circumstances personally is illustrated in a story about a fine leadership trainer. This trainer, a woman of great wit and presence, experienced a particular problem in every seminar she taught. Whenever she directed workshops and saw people leaving early, she automatically interpreted their departure as a display of disapproval. She wondered if they were leaving because she was too wordy. Perhaps she was too fat. Even worse, maybe she was a boring and inadequate presenter. She wasted a lot of energy and attention worrying about all these issues. She doubted her self-worth, and this turned an activity she loved into a frustrating and demoralizing experience. When she finally began to investigate this pattern of judgment objectively, she realized that people left workshops for all kinds of reasons, most of which had nothing to do with her. Objectivity helped her to see how easily she gave away her power, and it also created enough emotional distance for her to accept people at whatever level of participation they chose to demonstrate. Her ego no longer needed everyone to be a perfect participant.

Objectivity helps you view these kinds of experiences less personally, more dispassionately. You can pull out of habitual response and realize that even though you may experience some tough times, you don't have to be an emotional victim. And when you pull out of the drama and see it with new eyes, you can find a way out. Objectivity keeps you alert and open-minded, and can even help you discover gems of kindness or truth buried within the experience. When you aren't muddled in reaction and personal affront, you can perceive the exquisite details of living. You can see opportunities you didn't see before, and others will find you much easier to be with. Meditating won't take away responsibilities or problems, but it creates enough mental distance so you can view life with greater clarity, and as a result, act with more wisdom and less desperation.

Compassion

Another wonderful aspect of meditation is that it teaches compassion and tolerance. Compassion is not commiseration or pity. It is a merging of heart and head that allows real understanding and the ability to see both sides. Close-mindedness, inflexibility, arrogance — these qualities are devoid of compassion; their foundation is fear. It is fear that creates rigid definitions of what's right or wrong. When you're compassionate, you trust your inner confidence and are willing to be flexible because you don't feel threatened. You're willing to yield because you don't regard other ideas or people as adversaries. And most importantly, you're willing to accept the consequences of your compassionate actions, knowing that the integrity and generosity of your overall approach to life is well worth risking an occasional disappointment.

Through its generosity, compassion demonstrates security and courage. Emotional pain or fear is no longer a barrier to you. You see it as a dark cloud that passes, raining a lesson or a message. When you approach compassion with the strength of mindfulness (from Step 2, Centering), you can see fear's transparent curtain and push it gently aside. Think about what you could accomplish if you weren't stopped by fear!

Let's look at the quality of compassion by using an example of personal finances. We'll assume you are one of those individuals who can't get a handle on your money. Your savings account is empty, you're a compulsive spender, and your checkbook is never balanced. Are you willing to look squarely at how you manage money? You probably have some fear about this if you view money with shame and anxiety. And your fear is well-founded because the pain of self-judgment would surely throw you into despair and reactive spending. "Oh my God. Look at my bills, and look at how I've squandered my money. How could I have blown my savings like that? Boy, I'm really depressed. I'll just go out to dinner and to heck with it all."

Now, let's approach the same issue with compassion. Sure, you still feel some shame about it. But instead of harsh criticism and negative feedback, you use a different approach supported by the mindfulness you've learned in meditation. "Oh my God. Look at my bills. I haven't been handling my money wisely at all. Hmmm. I see some pretty negative judgment coming up about this. Isn't that interesting? Well, I can get depressed and spend more money, or I can try something else. These habits developed for a reason, but they certainly aren't serving me now. It may take time to change them, but I'll begin by balancing my checkbook this week."

In the business world, compassion keeps you in touch with your sincerity and your integrity. You maintain an enlightened, balanced view of the workplace, seeing that it's not only a place to get something from, but also a place to give something to.

Work becomes a stage, a playground for awareness and generosity of spirit. Work no longer defines you; it's simply another way to express yourself. Compassion gives meaning to your life and purpose to your daily actions. Every situation becomes an opportunity to live with a deeper, more profound sense of satisfaction — something that has been sorely missing from today's workaday world.

Objectivity, compassion, and tolerance are characteristics of people who are willing to learn from their shortcomings and to grow with the ever-changing world around them. Their lives are predominantly happy, successful, and productive. These characteristics, combined with a willingness to replenish your energy through moments of reflection, will not only make you happier and more pleasant to be with, but will also make you more efficient. And the by-product of efficiency is time — time to reevaluate your priorities, time to do what you want to do, and not always what you have to do, time to enjoy living now.

Timeout Sittings and Their Applications

Meditation will make a wonderful difference in your general approach to life. The ability to keep your heart and mind open brings new levels of emotional richness and joy into each day. But no matter how balanced and compassionate you become, there will still be times when stressful events catch you off guard. At these times you can inject a quick version of the MBP process into the situation. You can give yourself a booster shot of meditation by performing an MBP "timeout" sitting.

Unlike the standard form of MBP meditation, timeouts serve one primary function: They pull you out of automatic reaction and center you in the moment. They give you back your power. What you do with it is entirely up to you. You see, your true power doesn't rest in what you did in the past or what you plan to do in the future. The past won't change and the future hasn't happened yet. Your power for change is in the immediate moment, the now. Every moment is an opportunity to turn a new corner, try a new response, reinforce a new habit. Unfortunately, most of us don't know how to seize the moment because we're not consciously aware of it. We're distracted and bewildered by the mental onslaught of opinions, old responses, and fear of the future. We're not accustomed to witnessing an event, we only know how to get lost in our reactions to it. But our ticket to the present is a timeout sitting. When practiced, timeouts bring us back into the immediate situation and reconnect us to our power, our moment of choice.

The mechanics of timeouts are simple. You begin with the Step 2, Centering, process — using slow, deep breaths as your focal point. Next, you stop identifying with your current emotional state by removing the word "I" from your description of how you feel. For example, rather than say to yourself, "I am afraid," you could say, "Oh, here comes fear. Isn't that interesting."

These two tactics are deceptively powerful balancing tools. Deep breathing directs your attention away from the troublesome reaction and triggers the mindfulness you've developed during regular practice. This mindfulness helps you see that your immediate emotional condition is only a small (albeit loud) portion of your psyche. Removing "I" from the description of your emotional condition places you in a witness consciousness; that is, you watch what's going on rather than being part of it. When you witness your stress, you look at it with objectivity instead of behaving like a helpless participant. You do not flail around or get caught up in it. The witness part of you can take whatever positive action is appropriate. You have literally stepped out of the fire, and can now figure out how to douse it.

When you use a timeout to witness events and your reactions, you're not ignoring them, hating them, or rejecting them. You're merely stepping back to avoid an impulsive response, giving yourself room to assess the situation clearly. Surprisingly, a few seconds of sharp assessment can disrupt your habitual response and prevent destructive auto-reaction. The mind works so fast on so many levels that a few moments of clarity create a break in the reflex. The important point here is to learn the value of witnessing events, and then be able to "click in" to a witness consciousness when it is appropriate to do so. In a stressful work situation, during an argument with relations, or even while waiting at a lost baggage counter, your witness consciousness pulls you out of knee-jerk emotional responses. You can handle what is at hand without the added burden of overreaction and unclear thinking. Remember, this isn't a lifetime of emotional separation; it's only a few moments. But the speed of the mind can turn a few moments of clear consciousness into a complete change of attitude and behavior. Of course, there may be times when you don't want to use a timeout — romantic evenings, scary movies, therapy sessions, and so forth. But when you're in the middle of a circumstance that you want to handle in a new way, or if you would like to remain calm and clear during a stormy encounter, a timeout can make a big difference.

Don't be concerned if your first few attempts don't feel very effective. Changes in the habitual way you respond to life tend to be subtle. You usually don't get hit over the head with a new opinion or behavior. More likely, your new attitudes will emerge gradually, becoming more familiar and comfortable as you practice them. So don't be disappointed if you still feel the old tugs of habit for a while. Just because you feel them welling up doesn't mean they have to consume you. Through meditation, you can learn how to identify these tugging distractions as they arise and simply refuse to pay attention to them.

Timeout sittings allow you to exercise new approaches to old challenges. As you practice timeouts in conjunction with regular sittings, they become more powerful and their results more compelling. But even though the mechanics of timeouts are

the same in all situations, their surrounding circumstances require additional explanation.

At Work

The bulk of your waking time is probably spent
in some form of work or activity. It may be school,
office work, manual labor, or whatever. So it makes
sense that any new life-improving practice should
have direct application in the workplace. By meditating regularly, you become mindful of the dynamics of everything happening around you. Because you
know how to observe your thoughts without becoming confused by them, you can see your own reactions
as they develop and before you act. You know how to
manage yourself wisely and empathetically. People
begin to see you as an aware, confident individual who
views situations clearly and makes intelligent decisions. Discovering how to be comfortably tolerant of
your own mental machinations also makes you more
tolerant of others. You develop an inner peace and self-

confidence born of disciplined compassion, not brutal judgment. Unfortunately, even the most balanced meditator will experience events that can obstruct fair-mindedness in panic or stress. This is when a timeout can make a difference.

Let's use an example to illustrate the value of timeout sittings at work. Assume you're getting ready to make a presentation to an office superior or to a group. This could be a job interview, a progress report, or a sales presentation. Regardless of the circumstances, you feel anxious because you want to make a favorable impression. One way to accomplish this is to prepare for the meeting, stuff the anxiety into your neck or lower back until it is over, and then take two days to release the stress. That's how most people do it. Perform now and pay later. Although this method gets the job done, its overall effect is quite draining. Unrelieved stress is carried into your next work experience and eventually into your home. Tension headaches, short tempers, and sleepless nights become a way of life.

Another way to approach the presentation involves the same kind of preparation, but with the addition of a timeout before the meeting. You can sit in your car, in your office, or even in the restroom. Having meditated briefly beforehand, you deliver the presentation not only appearing calm, but you *are* calm. You may still feel the energetic rush that comes from doing something risky, but you won't waste your reserves in nervous anxiety. Even before the show begins, you're clear and alert. The result is the same good performance without the accompanying drain.

Pre-meeting timeouts work well for any planned event. But what about those unpredictable situations? You know, when you're quietly doing your job and suddenly you're asked to give a talk about your latest project, or answer questions about someone else's area of expertise, or meet with a person you really don't like. What then? You can still do a timeout. Right then take some deep breaths, focus on your breath, and witness your emotional state.

Instead of crying, "What am I going to do?" say, "Oh, there's fear. Isn't that interesting." Acknowledge that these feelings come and go. You've survived in the past and you will survive this time as well. You can do this at your desk, or while walking to the meeting. A good trick is to say that you'll be right there after a quick trip to the restroom. While walking, be mindful of your emotional whirlpool. "There goes exhilaration. And there's fear and anxiety, too."

Chances are that an extra two minutes isn't going to upset anyone's schedule, but those same two minutes can make an enormous difference in how you handle yourself. You'll respond more effectively when your mind isn't blocked in reaction. You'll be able to separate unreasonable fear, insecurity, or anger from your mental preparation. You may not win the Nobel Prize for diplomacy, but you'll be a lot clearer and your communication will come from a foundation of strength.

The best part is that the more you meditate, the better these timeout respites become. And the better you become at doing timeout sittings, the more energy you actually extract from challenging work situations. They are no longer depleting; they are invigorating. Will you still get nervous? Sure. Nervousness is a natural human response. But you won't be nearly as tense. Once you know how to be centered and calm, your body will respond automatically.

Personal Relationships

What is it about personal relationships that gets to you? Communication problems with your mate? Friends you don't really like? Do you turn into a ten-year-old whenever you're with your parents? Do you want to enliven and enrich an already good relationship, or do you want to repair a failing one? When you're dealing with another person and the circumstances are sensitive, overreaction (whether external or internal) can be one of your greatest problems. Reaction tends to build on itself, leading to layer upon layer of misunderstanding. Although you're bound to experience conflict on occasion, regular meditation makes you attentive and aware of your own emotional projections. You'll be less likely to overreact. This helps you actually hear what is being communicated to you, instead of blocking the connection with presumptions, time-worn defenses, and negative self-talk.

When it comes to relationships, even the most dedicated meditators can get lost in projected anger or old painful habits. As long as you have to deal with day-to-day living, there will be times when you're an argument looking for an outlet. But with the mindfulness you've developed from regular meditation, you can usually detect conflict-generating emotional states long before they spark any unpleasantness. When you feel irritated or annoyed with another person, you can catch yourself and perform a timeout.

For example, you may be late for some planned activity and begin to notice old emotions rising. You feel sensitive and defensive. Memories of unresolved friction get tacked onto current conditions. This is your window of opportunity for a timeout. You've identified your sensitivity before inflicting it on others. You begin to breathe deeply, taking a minute or so to redirect your attention away from the inner conflict. As you breathe, you can then observe your thoughts to see how past and present weave together. You watch your mind complicate immediate circumstances with issues such as wanting to be right, acknowledged, or reassured. As you identify the mental interplay, you separate from it, becoming conscious in the midst of your reaction and not lost in it. You are now in a powerful position to choose. You can be seduced by your frustration or you can look at those feelings, acknowledge their reasons for existence, and choose to deal only with the immediate issues.

This technique doesn't deny the validity of your feelings by stating, "Oh, simply choose to feel something else and you will." And this doesn't imply that anger, conflict, and other so-called negative emotional states are inherently bad and should be avoided. Anger is appropriate in a lot of situations and conflict is a natural part of companionship. Opening to negative emotions in appreciation of their rightful place allows them to serve their true purpose — as signposts and signals. Just as a stomachache tells you to look at your food consumption and a backache warns you to stretch during the workday, so do emotions such as anger and anxiety bid you to look deeper. They tell you to ask what is really going on. This means taking responsibility for your reactions, being attentive to them, and listening to them with interest and concern instead of denying them in fear and judgment.

It takes practice to be able to observe strong reaction without getting caught in it. And sometimes you just muddle through the best you can — getting caught, pulling out, getting caught, pulling out. Remember, there's always value in who you are and what you feel. Sometimes you'll get caught in a whirlwind, and stepping into objectivity will seem a distant dream. Lots of experiences in life can really try your compassion and objectivity to the limit, so you do the best you can, and when the drama subsides somewhat, you move on.

Granted, sometimes these feelings don't just pass you by. They stick. But the reason they stick is because you become so upset and anxious about them. "Oh no, I'm getting angry. Why does this always happen? Why do I always lose my temper? I hate this! Oh brother, I'm really mad now!" You actually fuel the emotion with expectation of its horror and misery. You become angry at the circumstances or the person triggering this awful experience and then angrier at yourself for being so obnoxious. When the emotional fire finally burns itself out, you feel miserable and guilty for being so unreasonable.

As you meditate more and more, you are less inclined to become lost in agitation. This means that you become capable of seeing the bigger picture, and when you see the bigger picture you are usually less reactive. You begin to see the interaction of emotions upon themselves and the habitual nature of their expression. You can acknowledge the appropriateness of whatever reaction is happening, if you feel it's justified, but you no longer see yourself consumed by it. You grow lighter, freer. In short, you become more aware of the unique circumstances surrounding every relationship and less inclined toward habitual response. Warmed by the compassion of an open heart, this kind of objectivity emanates from humility and courage. It takes humility to admit that old ways of responding just aren't working, and it takes courage to face the emotions and attempt a new approach.

Leisure Activities

Leisure activities are supposed to be fun and relaxing. When you plan vacations or take the day off, you expect to return refreshed. Sometimes it happens that way, but more often, the preparation anxiety combined with your everyday stress is so intense that it takes days for you to ease into a mind state that allows relaxation. Somehow, you're supposed to save all your tension for periodic release on Sundays and for two weeks out of the year. Further, because the mind responds to habitual patterns of thinking, you may suddenly lapse into anxiety-producing thoughts in the middle of a great vacation. At such times, instead of medicating yourself with an extra drink or wasting an afternoon in distress, you can do a timeout. Right there, you can trigger your mind back into the present moment, breathe into calmness and objectivity, and become clearheaded.

Much of your daily stress is created by unnecessary worrying about upcoming events. A certain amount of future planning is important, but you may carry it to the extreme and create a lot of anxiety with little to show for it. By developing the capacity to be mindful of your world, you learn to experience the here and now, allowing noisy, anxiety-filled thoughts to go their way. This makes a big difference in how you approach and enjoy your leisure time; you are better able to take full advantage of the break without wasting it in unnecessary mental clutter. You're not mentally a million miles away in some worrisome project.

Mindfulness and attention allow you to savor every moment of leisure that you have. It makes the joyous experiences even better because you are fully present. The food tastes wonderful, the beauty is intoxicating, the companionship is delightful, and the result is honest rest and relaxation.

Positive Expectations and Meditation

Positive expectations can make a difference in everything you do. Positive expectancy is the feeling that somehow, some way, things are going to work out for the best. When you practice positive expectancy, something bad may happen to you, but you approach it with the intention of learning from it or at least figuring out how to avoid it in the future. The end result is potentially positive, even if the situation itself is truly awful. Positive expectancy values your current experience in spite of appearances and looks toward healthy resolution.

"Okay," you say, "if I wanted a lecture about positive thinking I'd have bought some other book. What does this have to do with meditation?"

It's important to approach your new practice with an air of positive expectancy and interest, not the "Now I have to sit here and be miserable for twenty minutes," attitude. It helps to be willing to explore whatever comes up, to be inquisitive. "Hmmm. I wonder what I'll get to experience today. Sleepiness? Rapture? Distraction? Inner peace?" Every mental state has something to offer, something to teach. If you anticipate boredom or restlessness and become wrapped up in the dread, you may never find out what these states can tell you about your discomfort with change, your unwillingness to relax, or even your fear of success. Being positively expectant means that you are willing to consider the possibility that every experience has a gift for you.

Unfortunately, positive expectancy is often misguided and turns into unrealistically high expectations. In Western culture, many people believe that high expectations and demands for perfection are an asset because they demonstrate commitment. They're supposed to make you reach further, do the impossible, achieve the incredible. There's no doubt that demand for excellence is motivating. But taking it to the extreme — as working people often do — can also be a tremendous barrier. If your margin of error is too small and your judgments too harsh, you may not risk anything new. Or worse, you may give far too much power to your losses because you don't allow yourself to fully appreciate your gains. This leads to constant frustration, low self-esteem, and eventually results in emotional and physical exhaustion. You stop living. You give up on your dreams. You just put in time.

Healthy positive expectancy doesn't lead to this kind of depression. It doesn't support powerlessness, despair, or escapist fantasy. Positive expectancy promotes growth and success through honest self-appraisal, robust vision, and a respect for who you are and how far you've come. With this approach you can look squarely at your expectations, determine what is standing in their way, and then say, "I'm listening." You can make peace with your self-defined flaws because you're no longer afraid of them. Remember, it's difficult to change something if you're too busy judging it or denying it entirely. Your current habits developed for a reason. You may not know what those reasons are, but if you turn your back on them or try to force them into submission, they'll just be replaced by similar habits. To change them permanently, you have to remove judgment, make peace with their existence, and take caring action. You may feel uncomfortable with this idea and say, "Oh I know I compulsively overeat. But acknowledging my eating habits without judgment, and trying to come to terms with them — that's not easy. I'd rather force them out of existence because I can't stand looking at them." Have compassion for this discomfort. It does get easier. When you start opening to yourself, you'll begin to see how hardened and defensive you've become. It isn't easy to let go of all your defenses. You chip away the brittle layers of self-judgment a little at a time, using positive expectancy to keep yourself focused and moving forward.

Successful people will tell you that expecting to always meet or exceed high standards is irrational. Success and happiness come from trying your best, being tolerant of your mistakes, and then trying again. Productive, happy people meet failure with objectivity and don't let it stop them. They expect and tolerate mistakes. Failure becomes a lesson, not an albatross. People who succeed and enjoy their success also have compassion for shortcomings and don't let them get in their way. These individuals are flexible enough to view failures as messages guiding them into new and better ways to accomplish their dreams. "Ooops. That didn't work very well. Maybe I'll try it this way instead."

Working with Mental States

Positive expectancy leads to learning and growth regardless of the mental state you observe during meditation. Sometimes you may see things you don't like; you're not always going to enter meditation feeling fabulous. You may occasionally observe depression, anger, or fear. But when you meditate, you separate from the thoughts. Since you won't be swallowed up by them, simply watch and see what they have to tell you about yourself. Remember, if you give credence only to the surging spiritual highs and flatly reject the emotional lows, you're rejecting a large portion of your current expression of life.

Emotional lows teach you about yourself. They tell you about fears, misgivings, and unhealthy attitudes. When you look squarely at the lows, you can begin to unravel their complexity and decipher their code of communication. Essentially, you can learn what makes them tick. In meditation, you can practice observing them with compassion and addressing them with candor. And in the process of observation, you create enough distance to determine whether you want to continue in the low. The distance places you in choice, not in autopilot. You may not be able to disengage from every low you experience, but as you continue to meditate you'll be able to witness your feelings with greater objectivity. You can look at your state of mind, whatever its condition, and separate from it just enough to get back into choice.

As a meditator, you begin to understand the intricacies of emotional lows. You see how they build on themselves, and you get better at responding to the present situation without heaping the past on top of it. If you do act out negative feelings, you respond to your own reactions with compassion and mercy. Feeling bad about an experience and then learning from it is useful, but hanging on to the self-recrimination long after the experience is over serves no one.

Meditation helps you release the anguish with compassion. You do whatever you need to do to rectify the situation, and then you release it, acknowledging the learning you have received. Compassion validates you as a person even if you don't meet your own expectations. Compassion for emotional lows and mistakes comes from observation, responsible action, and ultimately forgiveness. The ability to let go and forgive is very liberating. It allows you to go on with your life, gain new understanding, and implement it wholeheartedly in your world.

The Expectation Trap

As a busy person, you are probably open to new and interesting ways to manage your world efficiently. It doesn't take much effort to find great ideas in the plethora of self-help books available. Most self-help books have a fair amount of good advice, but the problem is the unrealistic expectation that you should sustain the new pattern of thinking or performance with very few setbacks. This is the Expectation Trap.

You fall into the Expectation Trap by responding to mistakes and slips with unrealistic expectations. Instead of acknowledging your mistakes as temporary and even understandable, you reject yourself in anger and disappointment. You reinforce a deep belief that you really can't change, find happiness, or live a better life. And this book about meditation — or any other channel for personal growth and betterment — is turned into another reason to deny yourself appreciation and respect.

The Expectation Trap can be tricky because a certain amount of expectation is appropriate when starting any new practice. A model naturally forms in your mind. Ideally, the model provides guidance and instills motivation. More likely, it represents a standard that your own impatience uses to set you up for failure. The trap is set when you form a new set of expectations about who you should be without a real appreciation of the adjustments it takes to manifest permanent change.

It's tough. This culture cloaks success in very distant, high ideals. You live with these expectations all the time. And if the goal of professional, financial, and social success isn't enough, you then undertake meditation to compound your list of shoulds with perfect objectivity, discipline, and compassion. Whew! That's a big mountain to climb. It's a setup for complete failure. It makes going for change a very unpleasant prospect because the end result is always despair and defeat. Is this any way to approach something as gentle as meditation?

Meditation is a skill that takes time to practice. The rewards take time to integrate into your behavior patterns, so don't use this new practice to set up another unrealistic demand on yourself. If you lose your temper despite your practice, or feel frightened even though you did your breathing work, or miss your meditations for two weeks even though you scheduled them, don't worry about it. Returning to old, destructive behavior patterns is natural. Developing new patterns sometimes encounters resistance because you instinctively gravitate toward the familiar; known patterns aren't as scary as unknowns. If you become upset because you slip back into old habits, you're falling into the Expectation Trap. Instead of returning to well-worn paths of behavior and reaction, have compassion for that aspect of who you are. It's culturally ingrained, it's understandable, and with persistence it can be redirected into a more personally fulfilling and joyous response to life's ups and downs.

Forget about the media-inspired definitions of who you should be and how you should live. As you practice meditation, you'll find that living has more to offer than simply survival and competition. Through meditation you can learn how to appreciate and live with yourself. When you can live with your own self, you can approach other people with respect and objectivity. The rich imperfections of daily living become your highways to friendship, caring action, and inner peace. Through meditation you can learn how to effectively and thoughtfully navigate those highways, savoring the countryside as you travel. You illuminate your path and the paths of those you encounter. You exemplify the type of accessible strength, presence, and responsibility that a struggling world yearns to see. And one day, when some sensitive individual looks at your busy, happy lifestyle and says, "Maybe I can do it, too. Maybe I can learn to create sixty seconds of serenity no matter where I am or what I'm doing," then you've made a real difference. You've shared the wealth.

Congratulations. This is only the beginning.

APPENDIX 1

Reference Books

MEDITATION IS A GROWING, changing experience. You never learn all there is to know about it because as your mind opens and your boundaries expand, old information takes on new meaning.

Although *Meditation for Busy People* provides a good basis for starting your practice, it remains deliberately simple in many areas. The following books are excellent for advanced study as well as for general reading. This list is by no means a complete compendium of meditation-related books. There are countless other fine works available.

Minding the Body, Mending the Mind, Joan Borysenko, M.D. (Reading, MA: Addison-Wesley Publishing Company, Inc., 1987). An easy-to-understand book that explores healing the body through mindfulness meditation. The author is a Harvard Medical School instructor.

Journey of Awakening: A Meditator's Guidebook, Ram Dass (New York, NY: Bantam Books, 1982). An unpretentious book which dispenses useful philosophical tidbits and describes simple meditation techniques.

Seeking the Heart of Wisdom: The Path of Insight Meditation, Joseph Goldstein and Jack Kornfield (Boston, MA: Shambhala, 1987). A useful meditation manual born out of the author's twelve-year collaboration in teaching meditation retreats. Practices and exercises are included.

The Meditative Mind: The Varieties of Meditative Experience, Daniel Goleman, Ph.D. (Los Angeles, CA: Jeremy P. Tarcher, Inc., 1988). An overview of several meditation paths and their underlying philosophies.

The Three Minute Meditator, David Harp (Oakland, CA: New Harbinger, 1990). A simple, easy-to-follow handbook designed to help busy people take advantage of meditation "moments."

How to Meditate: A Guide to Self Discovery, Lawrence LeShan (New York, NY: Bantam Books, 1984). A sensible, straightforward approach to meditation.

Healing into Life and Death, Stephen Levine (Garden City, NY: Anchor Press/Doubleday, 1987). A comforting and insightful exploration of pain and grief. Exquisite sample meditations are included.

A Gradual Awakening, Stephen Levine (New York, NY: Anchor Books, 1979). A basic teaching text for meditation. Motivating and reassuring.

Nine-Headed Dragon River: Zen Journals 1969–1982, Peter Matthiessen (Boston, MA: Shambhala, 1987). A haunting, beautiful book about the author's spiritual journey from explorer/naturalist to Zen monk. Includes the history of Buddhism.

Emmanuel's Book, Pat Rodegast & Judith Stanton (New York, NY: Bantam, 1987). This book is about appreciating life and handling fear. Warm, comforting excerpts from Emmanuel's talks.

Zen Mind, Beginner's Mind, Shunryu Suzuki (New York, NY: John Weatherhill, 1970). Informal talks on the basics of Zen meditation.

A Gift for God, Prayers and Meditations, Mother Teresa (New York, NY: Harper & Row, 1975). A small, uplifting book of compassionate prayers and meditations.

APPENDIX 2

Common Questions

About the Author

DAWN GROVES is a minister, author, and educator. She is also a keynote motivational speaker well known for her dynamic teaching style, warm presence, and accessible wisdom. Dawn clearly addresses the challenges of people who are attempting to combine professional achievement, spiritual growth, and a balanced lifestyle. She teaches workshops and classes for the government, private industry, community colleges, and spiritual centers throughout the United States and Canada.

VISION ON A LAKE: *A Meditation Tape by Dawn Groves* Generate new energy and release old emotional and spiritual wounds through a gentle, richly visual meditative process. Narrated by Dawn Groves, each twenty-three minute meditation is accompanied by exquisite music which will enhance your unique inner adventure.

FOR INFORMATION about Dawn's lectures, workshops, classes, and tapes, please contact Dawn directly at:

Heron House
P.O. Box 5642
Bellingham, WA 98227

New World Library is dedicated to
publishing books and audio projects that
inspire and challenge us to improve the quality
of our lives and our world.

Our books and audios are available
at bookstores everywhere.
For a complete catalog, contact:

New World Library
14 Pamaron Way
Novato, California 94949

Phone: (415) 884-2100
Fax: (415) 884-2199
Or call toll-free: (800) 972-6657
Catalog requests: Ext. 50
Ordering: Ext. 52

E-mail: escort@nwlib.com
Website: www.newworldlibrary.com